Henry C Ripley
Saginaw City
Oct 16th 1865 Mich

Henry C Ripley
Saginaw City
Mich
Oct 16th 1865

BRYANT AND STRATTON'S

COMMON SCHOOL

BOOK-KEEPING;

EMBRACING

SINGLE AND DOUBLE ENTRY.

CONTAINING

SIXTEEN COMPLETE SETS OF BOOKS.

WITH

AMPLE EXERCISES AND ILLUSTRATIONS.

FOR PRIMARY SCHOOLS AND ACADEMIES.

BY

H. B. BRYANT, AND H. D. STRATTON,

PROPRIETORS OF "THE NATIONAL CHAIN OF MERCANTILE COLLEGES," LOCATED IN NEW YORK, PHILADELPHIA, ALBANY, BUFFALO, CLEVELAND, DETROIT, CHICAGO, AND ST. LOUIS.

AND

S. S. PACKARD,

RESIDENT PRINCIPAL OF THE NEW YORK CITY MERCANTILE COLLEGE.

NEW YORK:

IVISON, PHINNEY, BLAKEMAN & CO., 48 & 50 WALKER ST.

CHICAGO: S. C. GRIGGS & CO., 39 & 41 LAKE ST.

1864.

ELECTROTYPED BY
SMITH & McDOUGAL,
82 & 84 Beekman-st.

PREFACE.

THAT there is a demand for a primary work on Book-keeping, which, while it is specially adapted to the comprehension and wants of a younger class of students at our public and private schools, shall seek to enforce, in a philosophical manner, the abstract theories of the science, is assumed by the authors of this treatise, not solely as the basis of an apology for producing a new book, but as the result of careful inquiry among teachers and educationalists, not less than a faithful survey of the field of literature compassing this end.

Experience has often proven that less tact and labor are necessary in *discovering* a want than in *supplying* it, and the present effort whether or not the public may pronounce it successful, is made in full view of this fact. To state an abstract proposition, which the unerring testimony of figures will render impregnable is no difficult matter; but to give vital force to such a statement in clear and satisfactory analyses, whose sequences shall take a practical hold of minds not schooled in the processes of reasoning, is an undertaking which may well cause the conscientious author to pause upon the threshold of his well-meant endeavor. There are minds so constituted as to be able to grasp intuitively, and with unerring certainty, the grander truths of a mathematical problem, discarding alike the minor points of reasoning and illustration, and the pretentious "rules" which, though too often but diluted axioms, are kindly intended to aid the faltering steps of the less self-reliant; but these are the exceptions and not the rule; and hence, experience in teaching has shown us that in the majority of cases, the bare statement of a principle, however fundamental and vital, cannot be alone relied upon for the thorough work of instruction. The labor of a teacher is necessarily one of endless variety and repetition. "Line upon line, and precept upon precept" is the motto of his profession and the signet of his success. While it is not the privilege of an author to know, by actual contact, the individual wants of those whom he aims to instruct, he must, nevertheless be possessed of a general knowledge of these wants, and address himself conscientiously to the task of supplying them.

The authors of this treatise claim for it the distinctive merit of thoroughness, both in the statement and elucidation of principles. In its preparation, two points were assumed: first, that the class of students who would gather instruction from its pages were already learned in the idioms of their own language, no less than in the fundamental rules of Arithmetic; and second, that the teachers who would adopt it as a text book, would make themselves familiar with the general scope of its teachings, no less than the details by which its prime theories are enforced. In order that a text book should accomplish any certain result, there should exist a perfect understanding between the author and the teacher, each of which has his own peculiar sphere of labor into which the other cannot enter. The author deals in general principles and their most palpable applications, without being able to anticipate the particular and varied wants of the student, or to supply those wants, even if he knew them. The teacher on the other hand, is the living exponent of the dead letters and forms which, to unpractised eyes are surrounded with a mazy mystery which can be dispelled only by the human voice. His is the sacred office of an interpreter, the duties of which demand of him not only a thorough appreciation of the thought interpreted, but an intimate knowledge of the bearing and capacity of the mind to which he discloses the hidden lore.

In the multiplicity of exercises given, the teacher will find material for an almost indefinite variety of illustrations, and it should be his special care that the student be not permitted to pass from one set to another without fully mastering the subject, both in its general and special application.

The sets are short and definite in their purpose, the object being to keep constantly in view the *result* of the student's labor; for, while it is true that in no way can the science of Accounts be so quickly and thoroughly enforced as in showing at once the result of each separate transaction, as regards both the persons and causes affected, it is no less so that the fundamental theory of the science can best be made apparent by frequently exhibiting the *general* result of all the transactions.

The prominence which is given to Single Entry will, we trust, satisfy the public that we are not prepared to enter into the popular cry of authors and teachers that no system of Accounts is worthy of thought that does not fully carry out the test of equal debits and credits; for while we are free to express our decided preference for Double Entry, we cannot, either in justice to our own convictions, or the prejudices of the public, ignore the points of excellence, or fail to suggest such improvements as are deemed important to a system which *will be* used, to a greater or less extent, to the end of time.

In short, it has been the earnest aim of the authors to produce a book which, though its external appearance would not disgrace the shelves of the Bookseller, its internal merits will not permit it to remain there. It is a book designed for *use*, and as such is respectfully submitted.

BRYANT, STRATTON & PACKARD.

18 Cooper Institute, New York,
July 1, 1861.

CONTENTS.

PART I.—SINGLE ENTRY.

CONTENTS.

PART II.—DOUBLE ENTRY.

ABBREVIATIONS AND CHARACTERS

USED IN THIS WORK.

ABBREVIATIONS.

A

Ac't. . . . . Account.
Am't. . . . . Amount.
Ans. . . . . . Answer.
Apr. . . . . . April.
Ass't'd. . . Assorted.
Aug. . . . . . August.

B

Bal. . . . . . Balance.
B. B. . . . . Bill Book.
Bbls. . . . . Barrels.
B. Pay. . . Bills Payable.
B. Rec. . . Bills Receivable.
Blk. . . . . . Black.
Bo't. . . . . Bought.
Bro't. . . . Brought.
B. W. . . . Black Walnut.

C

Cap. . . . . . Capital.
C. B. . . . . Cash Book.
Co. . . . . . . Company.
Com. . . . . Commission.
Const. . . . Consignment.
Cr. . . . . . . Creditor.

D

Dec. . . . . . December.
D'ft. . . . . . Draft.
do. . . . . . . The same.
doz. . . . . . Dozen.
Dr. . . . . . . Debtor.
d's. . . . . . . Days.

E

ea. . . . . . . Each.
E. E. . . . . Errors Excepted.
Emb'd. . . . Embroidered.
Ex. . . . . . . Example.
Exch. . . . . Exchange.
Exp. . . . . . Expenses.

F

Fav. . . . . . Favor.
Feb. . . . . . February.
Fig'd. . . . . Figured.
Fol. . . . . . . Folio.
For'd. . . . . Forward.
Fr't. . . . . . Freight.

G

Gal. . . . . . Gallon.

H

Hhd. . . . . . Hogshead.

I

I. B. . . . . . Invoice Book.
Ins. . . . . . . Insurance.
Inst. . . . . . Instant.
Int. . . . . . . Interest.
Inv. . . . . . . Invoice.
Inv't. . . . . Inventory.

J

Jan. . . . . . January.

L

lbs. . . . . . . Pounds.
L. F. . . . . . Ledger Folio.

M

Mar. . . . . . March.
Mdse. . . . . Merchandise.
Mo. . . . . . . Month.
Mgy. . . . . . Mahogany.

N

No. . . . . . . Number.
Nov. . . . . . November.

O

Oct. . . . . . October.
O. I. B. . . Outward Invoice Book.

P

p. . . . . Page.
Pay't. . . . . Payment.
P. C. B. . . Petty Cash Book
Pd. . . . . . . Paid.
Pkg. . . . . . Package.
Pr. . . . . . . Pair.
pr., per. . . By.
Prem. . . . . Premium.

R

Rec'd. . . . . Received.
R. W. . . . . Rosewood.

S

S. B. . . . . . Sales Book.
Sept. . . . . . September.
Ship't. . . . . Shipment.
Sunds. . . . . Sundries.

Y

Yds. . . . . . Yards.
Yr. . . . . . . Year.

CHARACTERS.

@ . . At.
a/c . . Account.
% . . Per Cent.
$ . . Dollars.
¢ . . . Cents.
£ . . Pound Sterling.
s. . . . Shilling.
✓ . . Check Mark.
+ . . Sign of Addition.
— . . Sign of Subtraction.
× . . Sign of Multiplication.
= . . Sign of Equality.
$1\frac{1}{4}$ . . One and one fourth.
$1\frac{1}{2}$ . . One and one half.
$1\frac{3}{4}$ . . One and three fourths.

PLAN OF THE WORK.

THE course of instruction is synthetical, commencing at the foundation and working upward, making each principle and illustration the opening wedge to higher developments of reason and application, and enforcing at every stage, the *practical* bearings of the required labor.

The Book is divided into two parts, Part I being devoted to Single Entry, and Part II to Double Entry. Each part comprises *eight* distinct Sets of Books, four of which are written out in full, and four given in the form of memoranda for the student to arrange after the models given. The first Set in Part I is intended solely to show the use of the principal books, Day Book and Ledger. Set II begins to deal in *results*. Set III commences with a capital, representing a General Merchandise business, shows the use of the necessary auxiliary books, and enforces the theory of loss and gain by comparing the capital at commencing with that at closing. Set IV represents a Furniture business, introducing the necessary principal and auxiliary books. The peculiar feature of this set is the admitting of a new partner, and continuing the business in the same books.——Set. I, Part II, is purely initiatory, introduced for the purpose of enforcing the fundamental principles of the science. Set II continues the business of Set I, but enlarges it, and gives a wider scope of transactions, and more fully enforcing the theory and processes of producing results. This set is given in colors, as affording a more exact model for imitation. Set III contains the same transactions as Set III, Part I, and is presented for the purpose of showing the exact differences between Single and Double Entry. Set IV is a practical set, using all the necessary books of original entry as principal books; posting from them to the Ledger, dispensing with the Journal except for such entries as are not recorded in the other books. This set exhibits, in the most decided manner, the economy and symmetry of Double Entry.

The intermediate "Exercises for the Learner," and "Examples for Practice," are relied upon to make the theory and practice of the different sets effective. The "Practical Hints," at the close, embrace suggestions which should not be overlooked.

PART I.

SINGLE ENTRY.

PART I.

SINGLE ENTRY.

INTRODUCTION.

[1] In estimating the true basis of any science, it is well, if possible, to follow the line of its history, and become familiar with the order and processes of its development. [2] This is especially true of the science of Book-keeping, for although it is purely a branch of mathematics, and as such fully entitled to the favor and consideration of scientific men, yet at no period of its history has it ranked in the estimation of scholars, with the more complex and abstract sciences; [3] which fact is owing, mainly, to a misconception or under appreciation of its dignity and importance as connected with the actual duties of life. It is lamentably true that men will grow enthusiastic over the solution of a problem in Euclid, or the effect of a combination of movements upon a chess-board, who are ignorant of the first principles of this the most beautiful and practical of sciences; and are content to pass through life, receiving and appropriating the reputation belonging to men of science and erudition, while they are consciously and persistently unable to decide the simplest question in partnership settlements, or to appreciate the well-established theory of debits and credits in any of its practical applications or philosophical abstractions.

It is difficult to account for this strange inconsistency except upon the ground that Book-keeping is a *practical* science, and as such is suggestive of rude contact with actual business life. It has too much of "the smell of the shop," and mixes too promiscuously with unpoetic bales, boxes, and barrels. It is, doubtless, this restricted view of the science which, more than aught else, has deprived the world of sufficient data from which to compile its history, and left to the imagination and logical inference what had else been a connected series of recorded facts.

Necessity, it is said, is the mother of invention; and as all science is the immediate result no less of invention than investigation, it may with truth be said that science is the offspring of necessity. That the science of Book-keeping is essentially so will be apparent in the commonest application of its principles.

[4] The very condition of life is *want*, and the plans and purposes of life aim at the supplying of want. [5] This necessity of our being begets industry and frugality, and lays the foundation of all real progress in arts and civilization.

[6] To supply the necessities of life the earth, through careful and patient toil, is made to yield her abundance, and the various channels of human enterprise and skill are laid under perpetual contribution.

[7] The wants of man are so numerous, and the means of supplying them so various, that a system of mutual dependence and reciprocal labor becomes not only economical, but necessary; and thus, from the very first enforcement of the divine law, "In the sweat of thy face shalt thou eat bread," has there grown up a division and classification of labor and wealth.

[8] The tiller of the soil, whose products supply the necessities of hunger; the manufacturer of fabrics, which are to clothe the body; the artificer, whose cunning workmanship gratifies the more refined wants and tastes; the man of science, who supplies food for the mind; the spiritual teacher, who ministers to the higher development of soul faculties, and the common laborer, who lifts from our shoulders the drudgery of baser toil, are each dependent upon all the others for the sum of material and intellectual comforts which minister to their individual wants; [9] and a mutual *exchange* of these comforts constitutes the foundation principle and impulse of that grand system of economy which we call BUSINESS.

[10] To facilitate these exchanges it has been found necessary to establish some regular standard of value by which the comparative worth of commodities may be adjusted. [11] This standard is usually represented by certain precious metals, usually gold and silver, which also serve as a medium in effecting the exchanges. In all civilized countries this metal is divided into convenient particles, and stamped with its appraised value, and is used, either really, or by implication, in all commercial dealings.

[12] The particular necessity of Book-keeping is to preserve a record

of such exchanges as would otherwise be trusted to memory; although a thorough application of the science embraces other most important results. Its more simple and restricted use may be easily shown.

Suppose, for example, that John Smith is a farmer, and Thomas Jones a manufacturer; that John raises as much food on his farm as is necessary to supply his own wants and those of his neighbor, while Thomas makes clothing sufficient for the demands of both. It is now the easiest thing in the world for both John and Thomas to have food and clothing, simply by exchanging with each other their surplus products. [13] An exchange of this kind would possibly need no record; and were this the extent to which commerce had been carried, it is scarcely probable that obstinate brains would have been puzzled with the dry formulas of Book-keeping. But, suppose, further, that Thomas should happen to be in *immediate* want of some of his neighbor's surplus food, without the ability, *at the time*, to render an equivalent in his own products. He says to John, "I want food, and cannot pay for it now, but if you will confide in my honor, I will surely return you an equivalent when I have completed work now in progress." The conditions being satisfactory, the *food* is conveyed from John to Thomas, and the *promise* from Thomas to John. If John is blessed with a faithful memory he may be able to retain the facts connected with this transaction, and thus constantly bear in mind that he *owns* a certain quantity of clothing, which his neighbor is to bring him at a stated time. [14] But suppose he is not willing to trust to his own memory, nor to that of his neighbor, but desires something tangible which shall at least *represent* this prospective property—a *record* which will not fade with the memory, but will stand for the benefit of whom it may concern, even in the absence of those having a personal knowledge of the facts. The person relied upon to fulfill this promise is Thomas Jones, and [15] the most natural form of record would be to write his *name* in a book kept for that purpose, and state the fact underneath it, thus:

THOMAS JONES

Bought of JOHN SMITH, a quantity of food, valued at *Ten Dollars*, for which he agrees to pay a quantity of clothing of equal value, on [naming the date of payment.]

[16] A record like the above would be intelligible as containing all the facts, and affording to John Smith a tangible evidence of prop-

erty which he owns, but which is in the hands of another party; and if this single transaction comprised all of this nature it would scarcely be worth while to attempt a more concise or symmetrical record. [17] But as dealings of this kind may be very frequent, not only with Thomas Jones, but with other parties, it may be well to ascertain if some more satisfactory and less cumbrous method may not be adopted.

[18] The simple fact expressed in the foregoing record is that Thomas Jones *owes* John Smith ten dollars worth of clothing. [19] The only events which can vary this fact are, the payment of the debt, or a part of it, overpaying it, or adding to it by subsequent purchase without payment. [20] There are, really, but *two* conditions, as pertaining to persons with whom we have dealings on credit, viz.: that of *owing*, and *being owed.* [21] These two conditions are exact counterparts, and so far as they are equal, will cancel each other.

[22] It will, therefore, be easy to arrange these opposite facts under the names to which they pertain in such way as that not only the facts themselves, but their relative results, may be ascertained at a glance. For example:

DR.		THOMAS JONES.							CR.
Date.		*He owes us,*	*Dolls.*	*Cts.*	*Date.*		*We owe him.*	*Dolls.*	*Cts.*
1861 Jan.	1	To 1 Bbl. Flour.....	10		Jan.	15	By 4 yds. Cloth.....	10	
Mar.	1	" 10 Bush. Wheat.	12	50	Apr.	1	" Cash...........	5	

This form has been found by experience to be both comprehensive and practical. [23] It is called an *account*, and, as will be readily seen, [24] is a statement of dealings with Thomas Jones. [25] On one side are arranged the separate amounts of his indebtedness to us, and on the other of our indebtedness to him. [26] The *difference* or *result* will be a net amount owing either to us from Thomas Jones, or to Thomas Jones from us. In other words, if Thomas Jones owes us more than we owe him, the indebtedness is in our favor, and may be reckoned as a part of our property; while, if we owe him more than he owes us, the indebtedness is in his favor, and should be reckoned among our debts. The facts shown in the account given may be thus analyzed: [27] On the first of January Thomas Jones purchased of us 1 barrel of flour at $10; and on the 15th of January, sold us 4 yards of cloth for enough to cancel the debt. The amounts on the opposite sides of the account will now exactly balance each other, and the result is the same as though the exchange had been made at once. Again, on the first of March he purchased 10 bushels of wheat, for $12 50; and on the first of April pays us in cash $5. This leaves a deficiency in his account of the difference between $12 50 and $5; and we say that Thomas Jones *owes* us $7 50. We have thus a tangible record of property, which if left to memory might be forgotten, and we thus become losers.

[28] It will thus be seen that in all cases where exchanges are effected between parties, either of whom is allowed time to perform his part of the contract, some *written* record of the facts are necessary. [29] This written record constitutes the germ and sphere of Book-keeping.

From the foregoing illustration it will appear that [30] an account has two sides, a [31] *debtor* and a *creditor;* that [32] upon the debtor side is shown what is owing *to* us, and [33] upon the creditor side, what is owing *by* us; [34] that when the debtor side is the larger, the difference will express an amount belonging to us, [35] and when the creditor side is the larger, the difference will express an amount which we owe. [36] In the former case the account would represent property or resources; [37] and in the latter, debt or liability.

[38] In the earlier history of Book-keeping, doubtless this form, or something similar, was deemed sufficient for the purposes of trade, [39] it being absolutely necessary only to have some written evidence of such resources and liabilities as had no other tangible existence, and which it would be unsafe to trust entirely to memory. [40] It is evident, however, that in an extensive credit business, a book of *consecutive* record, giving a plain and simple account of the business as it progresses day by day, would be of essential service, and it is, therefore, the almost universal practice, particularly among merchants and tradesmen, to keep a [41] Day Book, in which are entered transactions as they occur.

An example, showing the form of this book, and also that of the Ledger, with the transactions properly transferred, will be seen on the following page.

DAY BOOK.

New York, January 30, 1861.

Jan.	30	John Smith, Dr. To 5 yds. Broadcloth.......@ $4 00 — $20 " 10 do Cassimere........@ 1 50 — 15 " 30 do Black Dress Silk.@ 1 25 — 87 50 " 25 do Flannel..........@ 50 — 12 50 " 10 do Figured Silk.....@ 1 50 — 15	100	
Mar.	1	John Smith, Cr. By Cash paid on account,	75	

These entries, carried to the Ledger, which is the Book of Accounts, would appear thus:

LEDGER.

Dr. John Smith. **Cr.**

Jan.	30	To Merchandise....	100		Mar.	1	By Cash..........	75	

42 The advantages of a Day Book are twofold: First, it affords a regular daily history of the business; and, next, by giving the particulars and details of each transaction in the Day Book, the *amount* alone may be carried to the Ledger, requiring thus less space, and preserving a more symmetrical form of the Ledger accounts.

43 The Day Book and Ledger in Single Entry contain only such transactions as relate to persons. 44 All prudent men, however, will feel the importance of having a strict record kept of the receipts and payments of cash and other people's notes, and of the issue and redemption of their own notes. 45 This is done by means of books specially arranged for such purpose.

The following are the most simple of these forms:

CASH BOOK.

			Received.		*Paid.*	
Jan.	1	Amount on hand..........	$3000			
		Received of James Monroe, on account................	150			
		Paid Store Expenses, as per Expense Book.............			175	
		Lent John Thompson for one day......................			500	
		Received of Jacob Schuyler for Bill of Mdse...........	75			
		" " Robert M. Hart " " "	18	75		
		Paid A. T. Stewart in full of account..................			400	
		Received for petty sales, as per Cash Drawer...........	110			
		Balance on hand............			2278	75
			3353	75	3353	75
	2	Amount brought down........	2278	75		

BILL BOOK.

Bills Receivable.

No.	When Rec'd.	Drawer or Endorser.	Drawee or Maker.	Date.	Time.	When Due.	Amount.		When and How disposed of.	
	1861			1860		1861			1861	
1	Jan. 1	Robert Minturn,	Jas. Cruikshank,	Dec. 1	60 ds.	Feb. 2	500		Feb. 2	Paid.
				1861						
2	" 5	Charles Hawley,	David Woods,	Jan. 5	30 ds.	Feb. 7	1000		Feb. 7	Paid.
3	Feb. 1	Abram Duryea,	Duncan Phyfe,	" 10	90 ds.	Ap. 13	1500			
4	" 15	W. W. Granger,	Ivison & Phinney,	Feb. 15	60 ds.	Ap. 17	300			

Bills Payable.

No.	When Issued.	Drawer or Endorser.	Drawee or Maker.	Date.	Time.	When Due.	Amount.		When and How Redeemed.	
	1861								1861	
1	Jan. 12	Samuel Higgins,	Ourselves,	Jan. 12	15 ds.	Jan. 30	150		Jan. 30	Paid.
2	Mar. 1	Peter Cook,	do	Mar. 1	90 ds.	June 2	750			
3	" "	John D. Hinde,	do	" "	60 ds.	Apr. 5	300			

These simple and suggestive forms comprise the books commonly used in Single Entry; and are, perhaps, sufficient for the most pressing demands of business record. It will be the aim of the instructions which follow in this part of the work, to present the subject of Book-keeping as expressed through the forms of Single Entry in as progressive a manner as possible; and with a view to prepare the mind of the student for the more perfect and beautiful science of Double Entry, which is unfolded in Part Second.

QUESTIONS FOR REVIEW.

1. How can the true basis of any science be best estimated? 2. Why is this especially true of Book-keeping? 3. Why has Book-keeping not usually been ranked with abstract sciences? 4. What is the chief condition of life? 5. What does this necessity beget? 6. How are the necessities of life supplied? 7. What system grows out of the numerous wants of man? 8. Name some of the classes of men who are mutually dependent one upon the other? 9. What constitutes the foundation principle and impulse of business? 10. How are these exchanges facilitated? 11. How is the standard of value represented? 12. What is the particular necessity of Book-keeping? 13. In the case cited between John Smith and Thomas Jones, where the food and clothing are simultaneously exchanged, is there any actual need of a written record? 14. In the case where the payment of the clothing is deferred, why is a written record necessary? 15. What is the most natural record of the indebtedness of Thomas Jones in the example given? 16. Would this record be intelligible? 17. Why is a more symmetrical and concise record necessary? 18. What is the simple fact expressed in the foregoing record? 19. How may this fact be varied? 20. How many conditions are there pertaining to dealings with persons on credit? 21. How are these conditions as compared with each other? 22. How may these opposite facts be best arranged? 23. What is this form called? 24. How may it be defined? 25. What facts are arranged on either side of an account? 26. What is shown by the *difference* between the sides of an account? 27. Will you analyze the entries in Thomas Jones' account? 28. In cases where exchanges are effected involving *time* in their fulfilment, what is necessary? 29. What does this written record constitute? 30. How many sides has an account? 31. What are they called? 32. What is shown by the *debtor* side? 33. What by the *creditor* side? 34. If the debtor side be the larger, what will the difference express? 35. What, if the creditor side be the larger? 36. What will the account represent in the former case? 37. What, in the latter? 38. In the earlier history of Book-keeping what form of record was probably used? 39. Why was this form alone sufficient? 40. What other forms become necessary in an extensive credit business? 41. What book is usually kept by merchants and tradesmen? 42. What are the advantages of a Day Book? 43. What class of transactions do the Day Book and Ledger in Single Entry contain? 44. What other records will all prudent men keep? 45. How is this done?

SET I.

(INITIATORY.)

DAY BOOK AND LEDGER.

SHOWING SIMPLY THE USE OF THE BOOKS, WITHOUT EXHIBITING
A GENERAL RESULT.

REMARKS.

In the following set we have the simplest forms known in Book-keeping, viz: [1] the Day Book and Ledger. [2] This set is designed to be purely initiatory, and is introduced mainly to exhibit the forms and character of these important books, which will be extensively used hereafter.

It must be borne in mind that [3] the true purpose of Book-keeping is to preserve a sufficient record of resources and liabilities, to enable the proprietor at any time to ascertain the condition of his business. [4] This purpose is only *partially* effected in the records which follow, but it is deemed important that this class of property and debts should be clearly understood before proceeding to the others.

[5] A Ledger, in Single Entry, is used to exhibit the relation in which the various *persons* with whom we deal on account stand to our business, and contains, therefore, only *personal accounts*, or accounts with persons. Inasmuch, therefore, as every entry on the Day Book is posted to the Ledger, [6] the Day Book, also, contains only records which pertain to persons.

[7] The Day Book records in Single Entry are direct and simple, first expressing the *name* of the person to be debited or credited on the Ledger, together with the *fact* of "Dr." or "Cr.," and next the consideration and amount. [8] These records are then transferred under the appropriate Ledger accounts, and thus exhibit [9] the *result* of the transactions, so far as persons are concerned.

The set here shown exhibits but few transactions, and those of the most simple kind, [10] and is not intended to show any *general* result of the business; the main object being to set forth the nature and process of the records which are to appear upon the Ledger.

The student is requested to note well the form and expression, that he may correctly render the "Exercises" which follow this set, and become prepared for the progressive labor in the succeeding sets.

DAY BOOK,—SET I.

New York, July 1, 1860.

1	*Robert Simpson,*		*Dr.*		
	To 10 lbs. Rio Coffee,	*@ 12¢*	*$1 20*		
	,, 1 ,, Best Black Tea,		*1 00*		
	,, 25 ,, Crushed Sugar,	*,, 12¢*	*3 00*	*5*	*20*
	,,				
1	*James Cruikshank,*		*Dr.*		
	To 1 Box Raisins, 25 lbs.	*@ 20¢*		*5*	
	,,				
1	*Horace Webster,*		*Dr.*		
	To 1 Gal. Vinegar,		*0 75*		
	,, 3 lbs. Black Tea,	*@ 75¢*	*2 25*		
	,, 4 Bush. Apples,	*,, 1 00*	*4 00*	*7*	
	2				
1	*W. L. Carpenter,*		*Dr.*		
	To 50 lbs. Ham,	*@ 11¢*	*5 50*		
	,, 1 Box Herrings,		*2 00*	*7*	*50*
	Cr.				
	By Cash on %			*5*	
	3				
2	*John Shields,*		*Dr.*		
	To 1 Bbl. Flour,			*8*	
	,,				
2	*Peter Van Wyck,*		*Dr.*		
	To 5 Gals. Cider Vinegar,	*@ 75¢*	*3 75*		
	,, 3 Bush. Potatoes,	*,, 1 00*	*3 00*	*6*	*75*

DAY BOOK,—SET I.

New York, July 5, 1860.

L.F.	Particulars		Amount	Total	
2	Peter Cooper,	Dr.			
	To 6 Gals. Molasses,	@ 75¢	4 50		
	,, 50 lbs. Sugar,	,, 12¢	6 00		
	,, 12 ,, Coffee,	,, 11¢	1 32	11	82
	6				
2	Stephen O. Hayward,	Dr.			
	To 1 Bbl. Mess Pork,		11 00		
	,, 3 Boxes Sugar, ea. 500 lbs,	@ 6¢	90 00	101	
	7				
3	J. B. Atwood,	Cr.			
	By Bill of Merchandise, per Invoice,			300	
	Dr.				
	To order on S. O. Hayward,			101	
	,,				
2	S. O. Hayward,	Cr.			
	By order as above,			101	
	8				
3	James Sweeney,	Dr.			
	To 100 lbs. Loaf Sugar,	@ 9¢	9 00		
	,, 50 ,, Crushed ,,	,, 8¢	4 00		
	,, 3 Hhds. Molasses,	,, $20	60 00	73	
	10				
3	F. R. Stebbins,	Dr.			
	To 1 Tierce Rice, 1800 lbs.,	@ 3¢		54	

Dr. Robert Simpson. Cr.

				$	cts.					$	cts.
1860 July	1	To Sund. Art.	1	5	20						

Dr. James Cruikshank, Cr.

				$	cts.					$	cts.
1860 July	1	To 1 box Raisins	1	5							

Dr. Horace Webster, Cr.

				$	cts.					$	cts.
1860 July	1	To Sund. Art.	1	7							

Dr. W. L. Carpenter, Cr.

				$	cts.					$	cts.
1860 July	2	To Sund. Art.	1	7	50	1860 July	2	By Cash,	1	5	

Dr. *John Shields,* Cr.

1860 July	3	To 1 bbl. Flour,	1	8							

Dr. *Peter Van Wyck,* Cr.

1860 July	3	To Sund. Art.	1	6	75						

Dr. *Peter Cooper,* Cr.

1860 July	5	To Sund. Art.	2	11	82						

Dr. *Stephen O. Hayward,* Cr.

1860 July	6	To Sund. Art.	2	101		1860 July	7	By ord. (Atw.)	2	101	

Dr. **J. B. Atwood,** Cr.

1860						1860					
July	7	Ord. on Hayw.	2	101		July	7	By bill of Mdze	2	300	

Dr. **James Sweeney,** Cr.

1860											
July	8	To Sund. Art.	2	73							

Dr. **F. R. Stebbins,** Cr.

1860											
July	10	To 1 Tierce Rice	2	54							

EXERCISES FOR THE LEARNER.

FIRST SERIES.

The following transactions are to be written up in proper form upon the Day Book, and from thence posted to the Ledger, as in the set preceding.

Memoranda.

Jan. 1. Sold H. W. Ellsworth on %, 5 Bbls. Flour, @ $10. Sold James Harper 6 lbs. Coffee, @ 11¢; 5 lbs. Black Tea, @ 75¢; Received Cash on %, $2. . . . . **2.** Bought of Geo. A. Crocker on %, 50 Bush. Apples, @ 50¢; 50 Bbls. Potatoes, @ $2 50. . . . . **3.** Sold Geo. H. Brown on %, 10 Bbls. Apples, @ 75¢; 3 lbs. Black Tea, @ 75¢. . . . . **4.** Paid Geo. A. Crocker, Cash on %, $100. . . . . **5.** Sold Abraham Lincoln on %, 2 Yds. Broadcloth, @ $3; 50 lbs. Sugar, @ 8¢; 30 Yds. Sheeting, @ 10¢. . . . . **7.** Bought of James Madison, on %, 10 Bbls. Potatoes, @ $2 50. . . . . **8.** Sold F. A. Perley, on %, 5 Bbls. Potatoes, @ $3; 10 Bush. Apples, @ 68¢. . . . **10.** Paid Geo. A. Crocker, Cash, $50. . . . . . **11.** Sold P. C. Schuyler, 10 Yds. Broadcloth, @ $5; Received in cash, $25. . . . . **12.** Sold Peter Cooper on %, 8 lbs. Coffee, @ 12¢; 3 lbs. best Black Tea, @ $1; 50 lbs. Crushed Sugar, @ 12¢.

QUESTIONS FOR REVIEW.

1. What forms are shown in Set I.? 2. For what is this set designed? 3. What is the true purpose of Book-keeping? 4. Is this purpose fully carried out in the exercises of Set I.? 5. What is shown in the Single Entry Ledger? 6. What does the Day Book contain? 7. What is the form of record in the Single Entry Day Book? 8. Where are these records transferred? 9. When so transferred, what do they exhibit? 10. Is there any general result shown in this set?

SET II.

RETAIL DRY GOODS BUSINESS.

DAY BOOK, LEDGER AND CASH BOOK.

WITH STATEMENT OF RESULTS AT THE CLOSE.

Business Prosperous.

REMARKS.

In this set we are enabled to arrive at more perfect and satisfactory results, and to carry out more fully the true purpose of Bookkeeping, [1] that of exhibiting, at any time, the condition of the business.

By the use of the Cash Book we compass a most important object, in [2] keeping a check on the receipts and disbursements of cash, and showing the amount on hand. [3] Of all the books used in business none is more essential than this; and no cautious business man will ever attempt to do without it. It is true, the amount of cash on hand may be easily ascertained at any time [4] by *counting* it; but [5] this process affords no test as to improper expenditures or omissions. [6] A faithful record of the receipts and disbursements of cash, however—the difference agreeing with the amount actually on hand—gives a degree of confidence, not only in reference to the cash transactions, but to the business generally, which can be secured in no other manner.

[7] A Cash Book, properly kept, will, at any time, show the amount of cash on hand; and for this special purpose is it introduced in this connection. The form here used, though perhaps not the best for general purposes, is extremely simple and easily understood. It is customary, in most business houses, to close up the Cash Book [8] at the end of each business day, and bring the balance down as a basis for the next day's transactions. [9] We have varied this plan to better suit our convenience, closing up each week during the first month's business, and only once in the next month. This is deemed sufficient for the purposes of illustration.

The particular advance which is made in this set over the preceding is more apparent in the statement which follows the Cash Book, and which will show, at a glance, the grand design of Book-keeping.

Nothing is more desirable in connection with business record than [10] the ability to exhibit *results* in a clear and unmistakable manner. To this end the learner should be taught to attach much importance to the *statements* given in connection with the various sets, and particularly to the principles deduced therefrom.

DAY BOOK,—SET II.

St. Louis, April 1, 1861.

1	Roberts, Rhodes & Co., (N. Y.) Cr.				
	By Mdse. per Invoice,			4000	
	″				
1	James Campbell, Dr.				
	To 10 Yds. Calico,	@ 12¢	1 20		
	″ 5 ″ Ribbon,	″ 20¢	1 00		
	″ 20 ″ Sheeting,	″ 10¢	2 00		
	″ 5 ″ Broadcloth,	″ 3 00	15 00	19	20
	3				
1	Lauren G. Thomas Dr.				
	To 15 Yds. Cassimere,	@ 1 00	15 00		
	″ 20 ″ Dress Silk,	″ 1 25	25 00	40	
	4				
1	R. B. Finney, Dr.				
	To 10 Yds. Vesting,	@ 5 00	50 00		
	″ Trimmings, etc.,		10 00	60	
	5				
2	David P. Johnson, Dr.				
	To 6 Yds. Flannel,	@ 50¢	3 00		
	″ 12 ″ Alpaca,	″ 1 50	18 00	21	
	″				
2	Isaac Stevens, Dr.				
	To 12 Yds. Dress Silk,	@ 1 50	18 00		
	″ 6 ″ Fine Broadcloth,	″ 4 00	24 00	42	
	6				
1	James Campbell, Cr.				
	By Cash on %,			10	

DAY BOOK,—SET II.

St. Louis, April 8, 1861.

2	Cyrus Wheelock, Dr.			
	To 25 Yds. 10-4 Sheeting, @ 75¢	18 75		
	,, 6 Pairs Ladies' Hose, ,, 1 00	6 00		
	,, 12 Yds. Printed Jaconets, ,, 15¢	1 80	26	55
	10			
2	Robert Demarest, Dr.			
	To 25 Yds. Black Doeskin, @ 2 00	50 00		
	,, 50 ,, Bleached Shirting, ,, 15¢	7 50	57	50
	12			
2	Cyrus Wheelock, Cr.			
	By Cash on %,		15	
	,,			
3	James Atwater, (per wife,) Dr.			
	To 1 Doz. Linen Hdkfs.,	6 00		
	,, 10 Yds. Cotton Damask, @ 25¢	2 50		
	,, 14 ,, Black Bombazine, ,, 1 50	21 00	29	50
	15			
1	James Campbell, (per daughter,) Dr.			
	To 1 Pair Lisle Gauntlets,	1 00		
	,, 12 Yds. French Calico, @ 15¢	1 80		
	,, 3 Doz. Satin Buttons, ,, 25¢	75		
	,, 8 Skeins Twist, @ 4¢	32	3	87
	16			
3	James W. Lush, Dr.			
	To 1 Yd. Black Satin,	2 00		
	,, Trimmings for Vest	1 50	3	50

DAY BOOK,—SET II.

St. Louis, April 17, 1861.

2	**Robert Demarest,** Cr.		
	By Order on S. S. Packard, to Bal. %,	57	50
	————— " —————		
3	**S. S. Packard,** Dr.		
	To Order as above,	57	50
	————— 19 —————		
3	**James Atwater,** Dr.		
	To 20 Yds. Linseys, @ 50¢ 10 00		
	" 30 " Corset Jeans, " 30¢ 9 00		
	" 1 Doz. Gents. Socks " 3 00	22	
	————— 20 —————		
3	**S. S. Packard,** Dr.		
	To 10 Yds. French Broadcloth, @ 4 00 40 00		
	" 50 " Globe Drills, " 13¢ 6 50		
	" 20 " Paper Cambrics, " 12¢ 2 40		
	" 15 " Cotton Damask, " 25¢ 3 75		
	" 30 " Cottonades, " 33¢ 9 90		
	" 6 Pairs Kid Gloves, " 75¢ 4 50	67	05
	——— Cr. ———		
6	By Cash,	50	

DAY BOOK,—SET II.

St. Louis, April 25, 1861.

L. F.					
3	John J. Howell, Jr.,		Dr.		
	To 10 Yds. Mixed Satinet,	@ 75¢	7 50		
	,, 6 ,, Cotton Drilling,	,, 10¢	60		
	,, 1 ,, Fine Satin,		2 00		
	,, 10 Skeins Twist,	,, 4¢	40	10	50
	— 27 —				
4	Amos Dean;		Dr.		
	To 6 Yds. Black Doeskin,	@ 2 00	12 00		
	,, 1 Doz. Linen Hdkfs,	,, 50¢	6 00		
	,, 6 Pairs Gents. Hose,	,, 25¢	1 50	19	50
	— 30 —				
3	James Atwater,		Cr.		
	By Cash on %,			20	
	— ,, —				
1	Lauren G. Thomas,		Cr.		
	By Cash in full of %,			40	
	— ,, —				
2	Isaac Stevens,		Dr.		
	To 14 Yds. Poplin,	@ 1 25	17 50		
	,, 1 Pair Kid Gloves,		1 00	18	50

DAY BOOK,—SET II.

St. Louis, May 1, 1861.

1	*James Campbell,*		*Dr.*		
	To 12 Yds. Brilliant,	*@ 25¢*	*3 00*		
	,, 35 ,, Blk. Bombazine,	*,, 1 50*	*52 50*	*55*	*50*
	2				
1	*R. B. Finney,*		*Dr.*		
	To 10 Yds. Blk. Doeskin,	*@ 1 63*	*16 30*		
	,, 25 ,, Brown Sheetings,	*,, 12¢*	*3 00*		
	,, 20 ,, Check Gingham,	*,, 20¢*	*4 00*	*23*	*30*
	5				
1	*Roberts, Rhodes & Co.,*		*Dr.*		
	To Cash, (Dft. on New York,) on a/c,			*2000*	
	6				
3	*S. S. Packard,*		*Dr.*		
	To 15 Yds. Duck Drilling,	*@ 20¢*	*3 00*		
	,, 10 ,, Brown ,,	*,, 30¢*	*3 00*		
	,, 6 Pairs Pearl Spun Hose,	*,, 75¢*	*4 50*	*10*	*50*
	7				
2	*David P. Johnson,*		*Dr.*		
	To 8 Yds. Broadcloth,	*@ 4 00*	*32 00*		
	,, 10 ,, Doeskin,	*,, 2 00*	*20 00*		
	,, 1 ,, Satin,		*2 00*		
	,, Trimmings,		*5 00*	*59*	
	,,				
2	*Robert Demarest,*		*Dr.*		
	To 14 Yds. Dress Silk,	*@ 2 00*		*28*	

DAY BOOK,—SET II.

St. Louis, May 9, 1861.

4	*Robert C. Spencer,*		*Dr.*		
	To 10 Yds. Flannel,	*@ 50¢*	*5 00*		
	,, 6 Linen Hdkfs.,	*,, 38¢*	*2 28*		
	,, 20 Yds. Brown Sheeting,	*,, 12¢*	*2 40*	*9*	*68*
	10				
2	*Isaac Stevens,*		*Cr.*		
	By Cash on %,			*30*	
	12				
1	*R. B. Finney,*		*Dr.*		
	To 6 Pairs Gents. Hose,	*@ 25¢*	*1 50*		
	,, 1 Pair Suspenders,		*1 00*		
	,, 1 ,, Kid Gloves,		*75*	*3*	*25*
	15				
1	*James Campbell,*		*Dr.*		
	To 10 Yds. Broadcloth,	*@ 4 00*	*40 00*		
	,, 6 ,, Doeskin,	*,, 2 00*	*12 00*	*52*	
	,,				
1	*R. B. Finney,*		*Cr.*		
	By Cash on %,			*25*	
	20				
3	*John J. Howell, Jr.,*		*Dr.*		
	To 4 Yds. Beaver Cloth,	*@ 3 00*	*12 00*		
	,, 1 ,, Satin,		*4 00*		
	,, Trimmings for Coat and Vest,		*8 00*	*24*	
	21				
2	*Cyrus Wheelock,*		*Cr.*		
	By Cash in full of %,			*11*	*55*

DAY BOOK,—SET II.

St. Louis, May 25, 1861.

L. F.	Particulars	Rate	Items	Dollars	Cents
1	*R. B. Finney,* Cr.				
	By Cash to balance %,			61	55
	— 27 —				
3	*John F. Howell, Jr.,* Cr.				
	By 2 Cords Wood,	@ 5 00	10 00		
	,, 50 lbs. Butter,	,, 16¢	8 00	18	
	— ,, —				
3	*James W. Lusk,* Dr.				
	To 13 Yds. Mous. de Laine,	@ 25¢	3 25		
	,, 14 ,, Figured Silk,	,, 1 50¢	21 00		
	,, Trimmings for Dress,		10 00	34	25
	— 28 —				
4	*Robert C. Spencer,* Dr.				
	To 12 Yds. Broadcloth,	@ 4 00	48 00		
	,, 6 ,, Black Doeskin,	,, 2 00	12 00	60	
	— 30 —				
4	*Amos Dean,* Dr.				
	To 50 Yds. Brown Sheeting,	@ 12¢	6 00		
	,, 10 ,, Pressed Flannel,	,, 75¢	7 50	13	50
	— Cr. —				
4	By Cash in full of %,			33	

INDEX TO LEDGER,—SET II.

A	**N**
Atwater, James, 3	
B	**O**
C	**P**
Campbell, James, 1	*Packard, S. S.,* 3
D	**Q**
Demarest, Rob't, 2 *Dean, Amos,* 4	
E	**R**
	Roberts, Rhodes, & Co., 1
F	**S**
Finney, R. B., 1	*Stevens, Isaac,* 2 *Spencer, Rob't C.,* 4
G	**T**
	Thomas, L. G., 1
H'	**U**
Howell, J. J., Jr., 3	
I J	**V**
Johnson, David P., 2	
K	**W**
	Wheelock, Cyrus, 2
L	**X Y**
Lusk, James W., 3	
M	**Z**

Dr. Roberts, Rhodes & Co. Cr.

1861						1861				
May	5	To Cash,	4	2000		Apr.	1	By Mdse., 4000 / 2000 / 2000	1	4000

Dr. James Campbell. Cr.

1861						1861				
Apr.	1	To Mdse.,	1	19	20	Apr.	6	By Cash,	1	10
,,	15	,, ,,	2	3	87					
May	1	,, ,, 130 57 / 10	4	55	50					
,,	15	,, ,, 120 57	5	52						

Dr. Lauren G. Thomas. Cr.

1861						1861				
Apr.	3	To Mdse.,	1	40		Apr.	30	By Cash,	4	40

Dr. R. B. Finney. Cr.

1861						1861					
Apr.	4	To Mdse.,	1	60		May	15	By Cash,		25	
May	2	,, ,,	4	23	30	,,	25	,, ,,		61	55
,,	12	,, ,,	5	3	25						
				86	55					86	55

LEDGER,—SET II.

Dr. David P. Johnson. Cr.

1861											
Apr.	5	To Mdse.,	1	21							
May	7	" " 80 00	5	59							

Dr. Isaac Stevens. Cr.

1861						1861					
Apr.	5	To Mdse.,	1	42		May	10	By Cash,	6	30	
"	30	" " 60 50 / 30 / 30 50	4	18	50						

Dr. Cyrus Wheelock. Cr.

1861						1861					
Apr.	8	To Mdse.,	2	26	55	Apr.	12	By Cash,	2	15	
						May	21	" "	6	11	55
				26	55					26	55

Dr. Robert Demarest. Cr.

1861						1861					
Apr.	10	To Mdse.,	2	57	50	Apr.	17	Order S. S. P.	3	57	50
May	7	" " 85 50 / 57 50 / 28 00	5	28							

Dr. James Atwater, Cr.

1861						1861				
Apr.	12	To Mdse.,	2	29	50	Apr.	30	By Cash,	4	20
,,	19	,, ,,	3	22						
		51 50 20 31 50								

Dr. James W. Lusk, Cr.

1861										
Apr.	16	To Mdse.,	2	3	50					
May	27	,, ,,	7	34	25					
		37 75								

Dr. S. S. Packard, Cr.

1861						1861				
Apr.	17	To D.'s order,	2	57	50	Apr.	20	By Cash,	3	50
,,	20	To Mdse.,	3	67	05					
May	6	,, ,,	4	10	50					
		135 05 50 85 05								

Dr. John J. Howell, Jr., Cr.

1861						1861				
Apr.	25	To Mdse.,	4	10	50	May	27	By Sundries	7	18
May	20	,, ,,	6	24						
		34 50 18 16 50								

Dr. Amos Dean. Cr.

1861						1861					
Apr.	27	To Mdse.	4	19	50	May	30	By Cash,		33	
May	3	" "	7	13	50						
				33						33	

Dr. Robert C. Spencer, Cr.

1861											
May	9	To Mdse.	5	9	68						
"	28	" " 69 68	7	60							

CASH BOOK,—SET II.

Cash,

			Dr.		Cr.	
1861 Apr.	1	Amount on hand,	1500			
		Paid for Station'y, Post. stamps, etc.			8	
		Received for Sales this day, per tickets,	115	25		
	2	Paid for Insurance, ½% on $4000,			20	
		,, Drayage on Mdse.,			5	
		Received for Sales this day, per tickets,	175			
	3	Drew out for Personal Expenses,			15	
		Paid Porter on % of Wages,			5	
		Received for Sales this day, per tickets,	87	23		
	4	Paid Expenses Cleaning Store,			2	50
		,, for 1 Box Pens,				88
		Received for Sales this day, per tickets,	110	50		
	5	Paid for Letter Press,			7	50
		,, ,, putting Light in Window,			2	50
		Received for Sales this day, per tickets,	183	25		
	6	,, of James Campbell on %,	10			
		Paid Clerk's Salary,			15	
		Received for Sales this day, per tickets,	100			
		Balance on hand,			2199	85
			2281	23	2281	23
	8	Balance brought down,	2199	85		
		Paid for 1 Doz. Balls Twine,			1	20
		,, ,, Carriage Hire,			4	
		Received for Sales this day, per tickets,	215			
	9	Paid Drayage, $4; Porterage, $3,			7	
		,, for Show Case,			20	
		Carried over,	2414	85	32	20

CASH BOOK,—SET II.

		Cash,	Dr.		Cr.	
1861 Apr.		Brought over,	2414	85	32	20
		Received for Sales this day, per tickets,	76			
	10	Paid for Safe,			250	
		,, Book-keeper on %,			10	
		,, Small items of Expense,			1	28
		Received for Sales this day, per tickets,	110			
	11	Paid Rent in full to May 31,			200	
		,, on Bill of Furniture,			25	
		Received for Sales this day, per tickets,	76	75		
	12	,, of Cyrus Wheelock, on %,	15			
		,, for Sales this day, per tickets,	84			
	13	,, ,, ,, ,,	98	75		
		Balance on hand,			2356	87
			2875	35	2875	35
	15	Balance brought down,	2356	87		
		Paid Express Charges,			1	50
		,, for Postage Stamps,			1	
		,, Carpenter for Repairing Store,			56	83
		Received for Sales this day, per tickets,	95			
	16	,, ,, ,, ,,	88	75		
	17	,, ,, ,, ,,	126	31		
	18	Paid Drayage, $4; Freight, $7 50,			11	50
		Received for Sales this day, per tickets,	175			
	19	,, ,, ,, ,,	210	50		
	20	,, of S. S. Packard on %,	50			
		,, for Sales this day,	112	81		
		Balance on hand,			3144	41
			3215	24	3215	24

CASH BOOK,—SET II.

		Cash,	*Dr.*		*Cr.*	
1861						
Apr.	22	Balance on hand,	3144	41		
		Paid for 2 Tons Coal, @ $5 00,			10	
		,, Balance on Furniture,			53	
		Received for Sales this day, per tickets,	103	20		
	23	,, ,, ,, ,,	129			
	24	,, ,, ,, ,,	180	58		
	25	Paid Book-keeper on %,			15	
		Received for Sales this day, per tickets,	98			
	26	,, ,, ,, ,,	163	75		
	27	Paid Drayage,			10	
		,, Porterage,			6	
		Received for Sales this day, per tickets,	173	81		
		Balance on hand,			3898	75
			3992	75	3992	75
	29	Balance brought down,	3898	75		
		Paid Express Charges on Package from Chicago,			1	50
		,, Freight on Mdse.,			24	75
		Received for Sales this day, per tickets,	74	10		
	30	,, of James Atwater, on %,	20			
		,, ,, L. G. Thomas, in full,	40			
		,, for Sales this day, per tickets,	125			
		Balance on hand,			4131	60
			4157	85	4157	85

CASH BOOK,—SET II.

Cash, Dr. Cr.

			Dr. $	¢	Cr. $	¢
1861						
May	1	Balance on hand,	4131	60		
		Paid for Firkin of Butter for Family,			10	
	2	,, for Stationery,			1	50
	5	,, Roberts, Rhodes & Co. on %,			2000	
	7	,, Clerk's Salary,			50	
		Received for Sales this Week,	497	84		
	10	,, of Isaac Stevens, on %,	30			
	12	Paid for Inv. Mdse., Freight, etc.,			1575	88
		,, on % of Rent,			50	
		,, for Carriage Hire,			15	
	14	Received for Sales this Week,	553	25		
	15	,, of R. B. Finney on %,	25			
	17	Paid for Ton of Hay,			12	
	20	,, Gas Bill,			10	24
	21	Received of Cyrus Wheelock, in full of %,	11	55		
		,, for Sales this Week,	723	85		
	25	,, of R. B. Finney, in full of %,	61	55		
	26	Paid for Postage Stamps,			3	
		,, ,, Stationery,			5	
	28	Received for Sales this Week,	573	24		
	30	,, of Amos Dean, in full of %,	33			
		Balance on hand,			2908	26
			6640	88	6640	88
		Balance on hand,	2908	26		

STATEMENT.

[11] THE facts embraced in the following statement are gathered from the preceding Ledger and Cash Book, and will afford a more concise and satisfactory view of the true purport of Book-keeping than could be enforced by any other form of argument. [12] It must be borne in mind that any statement which shows the *condition* of business must embrace a list of its property and debts; or, in business language, its *resources* and *liabilities;* and, consequently, [13] any system of Book-keeping which will enable one the most easily and certainly to get at these facts, must—other things being equal—be the best system.

The variety of resources and liabilities in the business here represented is quite limited, and requires, therefore, fewer aids than would otherwise be essential. In fact, the Cash Book and Ledger, in connection with an inventory of unsold merchandise, afford all the necessary results for the purposes of a statement.

Resources.				
1. *From Ledger Accounts.*—[14] Balances due from persons.				
James Campbell,	$120	57		
David P. Johnson,	80	00		
Isaac Stevens,	30	50		
Robert Demarest,	28	00		
James Atwater,	31	50		
James W. Lusk,	37	75		
S. S. Packard,	85	05		
John J. Howell, Jr.,	16	50		
Robert C. Spencer,	69	68		
2. *From Cash Book.*—[15] Balance of Cash on hand,	2908	26		
3. *From Inventory.*—[16] Merchandise on hand*.	1075	45	$4483	26
Liabilities.				
[17] *From Ledger Accounts.*—Balance due Roberts, Rhodes & Company,			2000	
PRESENT WORTH,			$2483	26

* The value of merchandise on hand has necessarily to be assumed. In business it would be ascertained by taking an actual inventory or "Account of stock."

STATEMENT.

From the foregoing abstract we ascertain the present worth or net capital of the concern to be, ...	$2483 26
From which, if we deduct the investment at commencing,	1500
We shall show the net gain during the two months to be,	$983 26

From these illustrations we gather the following

RULES.

18 **1.** *To ascertain the* NET CAPITAL, *or* PRESENT WORTH, *subtract the liabilities from the resources.*

19 **2.** *To ascertain the* NET GAIN *during business, subtract the net capital at commencing from the net capital at closing.*

EXAMPLES FOR PRACTICE.

THE following examples are given to make the student more familiar with the principles embraced in the preceding set; and especially to enforce the theory of the foregoing rules. He should be required, not only to produce the proper results, but in each case to render a *written statement*, similar to that on the preceding page.

EXAMPLE I.—A merchant commenced business with a capital of $5000. At the end of the year he gathers from his books the following facts: Amount of Cash received, $15,000; Amount paid out, $10,500; A. B.'s account stands, Dr. $1500; Cr. $1000; C. D.'s, Dr. $4000; Cr. $3500; E. F.'s, Dr. $975; Cr. $450; G. H.'s, Dr. $483 75; Cr. $300; Merchandise on hand, as per inventory, $2750; Amount owing to J. K., $1500. *Required, the net capital at closing, and the net gain during business.*

EXAMPLE II.—A. and B. commence business with the following resources: Cash, $3000; Notes, $1500; Merchandise, $3500; Real Estate, $10,000; Balance due on personal accounts, $12,500. At the end of six months, their resources and liabilities are as follows: Cash on hand, $1500; Cash in Bank, $4000; Notes, $3500; Merchandise, $3750; Real Estate, $15,000; Due on Personal Accounts, $5000;—Amount due from the firm, on their notes, $750; Amount due to persons on account, $1500. *Required, the capital at commencing; at closing; and the net gain.*

EXERCISES FOR THE LEARNER.

SECOND SERIES.

THE following transactions should be written up with great care. Let the student use *all* the books introduced in Set II., and in the same manner.

Memoranda.

July 1. Commenced Business with Cash on hand, $1500.—Bo't of Harrison Scott on %, 50 Bbls. Genesee Flour, @ $8; 2 Hhds. Molasses, 140 Gals., @ 40¢; 12 Boxes Soap, @ $4; 6 Half Chests Y. H. Tea, @ $20.—Paid for Stationery and Sundry Expenses, $50. —Rec'd Cash, for Petty Sales, $15.—**2.** Sold J. W. Husted, on %, 10 Bbls. Genesee Flour, @ $9 25; 4 Boxes Soap, @ $4 25.—Paid Drayage, $2.—Rec'd Cash for Petty Sales, $50.—**3.** Sold John Banks on %, 15 Bbls. Flour, @ $9 50; 3 Half Chests Tea, @ $25.—Paid Harrison Scott, Cash on %, $200.—Rec'd Cash for Petty Sales, $75.—**4.** Bo't of Henry P. Smith, on %, 10 Hhds. Molasses, 1200 Gals., @ 50¢; 12 Boxes Havana Sugar, 3750 lbs., @ 6¢.—Sold J. C. Hall, on %, 10 Gals. Molasses, @ 75¢; 1 Bbl. Flour, @ $9.—Rec'd Cash for Petty Sales, $110.—**5.** Sold Henry P. Smith, on %, 5 Bbls. Flour, @ $9.—Received Cash on % of John Banks, $50.—Rec'd Cash for Sales this day, $115 75.—**6.** Paid Cash for Stationery, $5 50.—Rec'd Cash for Sales this day, $110 75.—**8.** Bo't of C. J. Judd, on %, 5 Bbls. Coffee Sugar, 1000 lbs., @ $6\frac{1}{2}$¢; 6 Hhds. Molasses, 4000 Gals., @ 50¢.—Rec'd Cash for Sales this day, $75 50.—**9.** Paid Cash for Clerk Hire, $50.—Received for Sales this day, $50.—**10.** Rec'd Cash for Sales this day, $83 30.—**11.** Sold John Banks, on %, 10 Gals. Molasses, @ 60¢; 50 lbs. Coffee Sugar, @ 7¢; 1 Bbl. Flour, @ $9.—Rec'd Cash for Sales this day, $68 50.—**12.** Paid C. J. Judd Cash on %, $500.—Rec'd Cash for Sales this day, $75. —**13.** Rec'd Cash for Sales this day, $117 50.—**15.** Bo't of Thomas Palmer on %, 3 Bbls. Soda Crackers, @ $4 20; 12 Boxes Butter Crackers, 360 lbs., @ 6¢; 40 Loaves Bread, @ 10¢.—Paid Porterage in Cash, $3; For Cleaning Store, $5.—Rec'd Cash for Sales this day, $123 75.—**16.** Paid James Smith, Cash for Repairing Store, $25.—Sold Rob't Hayward, on %, 1 Bbl. Soda Crackers, @ $5; 3 Boxes Butter Crackers, 90 lbs., @ 7¢.—Rec'd Cash for Sales this day, $97 50.—**17.** Rec'd Cash for Sales this day, $125 75.—**18.** Sold W. F. Norman on %, 100 lbs. Sugar, @ 7¢; 50 Gals. Molasses, @ 60¢; 60 lbs. Sugar, @ 7¢.—Paid Smith & McDougal for Printing Circulars, $5 50.—Rec'd Cash for Sales this day, $88 93.—**19.** Paid Cash for Postage Stamps, $3; Letter Paper, $5.—Rec'd Cash for Sales this day, $98 37.—**20.** Rec'd Cash for Sales this day, $117 95.—**22.** Rec'd Cash on % of John Banks, $50.—Sold Robert Hayward on %, 30 Gals. Molasses, @ 60¢; 2 H'f Chests Tea, @ $25.—Rec'd Cash for Sales this day, $84 28.—**23.** Rec'd Cash on % of Rob't Hayward, $30.—Rec'd Cash for Sales this day, $75.—**24.** Sold J. C. Buttre on %, 1 Hhd. Molasses, 75 Gals., @ 56¢.—Rec'd for Sales this day, $65 75.—**25.** Rec'd Cash of Rob't Hayward, in full of %, $49 30.—Rec'd Cash for Sales this day, $78 25.—**26.** Rec'd Cash for Sales this day, $48 95.—**27.** Paid Clerk's Salary in Cash, $50.—Rec'd Cash on % of J. C. Hall, $16 50.—Paid Henry P. Smith, Cash in full of %, $780.—Rec'd Cash for Sales this day, $81 38.—Mdse. unsold, amounts, per Inventory, to $1500.

QUESTIONS FOR REVIEW.

REMARKS, PAGE 28.

1. What more perfect results are shown in Set II? 2. What important end is accomplished in keeping a Cash Book? 3. What is one of the most essential books in business? 4. How may the amount of cash on hand be ascertained without the use of a Cash Book? 5. What tests are omitted if we depend solely upon *counting* the cash? 6. What advantages are there in a faithful record of receipts and disbursements of cash? 7. What will be shown at any time by a Cash Book properly kept? 8. How often in business is it customary to close up the Cash Book? 9. How often is the Cash Book, used in this connection, closed? 10. What is a desirable feature in business record?

STATEMENT, PAGE 45.

11. From what sources are the facts exhibited in the Statement on page 43 obtained? 12. What is an indispensable requisite to any statement showing the condition of business? 13. What is the sure test of superiority in a system of Book-keeping? 14. What class of resources are found in the Ledger? 15. What, in the Cash Book? 16. What ascertained only from Inventory? 17. How are our liabilities ascertained? 18. What is the rule for ascertaining the *present worth* of a concern? 19. What, for ascertaining the *gain during business?*

SET III.

WHOLESALE DRY GOODS BUSINESS.

(PARTNERSHIP.)

DAY BOOK, LEDGER, SALES BOOK, CASH BOOK, AND BILL BOOK.

WITH STATEMENT OF AFFAIRS AT THE COMMENCEMENT, AND ALSO AT THE CLOSE.

Business Adverse.

REMARKS.

In the set which follows we have enlarged the area of our labor, by enlarging our business, and adding somewhat to the variety of our resources and liabilities. The peculiar feature of this set consists in the auxiliary books, which are introduced for the double purpose of teaching their use, and preserving a more complete record of the transactions. The form of Cash Book given in this connection differs from that in Set II, in its arrangement of receipts and payments. This form is the one in common use, and is preferable to the other, mainly on account of its complete separation of the two conditions named; the *receipts* being placed on one page, and the *payments* on the other. The Bill Book and Sales Book will explain themselves. There are more comprehensive forms for the Bill Book in use, but the form here submitted is the one more generally used, and has the merit of simplicity and plainness. The Sales Book is one of the most convenient auxiliaries a merchant can adopt; and particularly where any amount of wholesaling or general credit business is done. It is not absolutely essential that the credit sales should be entered on the Day Book, as they may easily be posted from the Sales Book direct; but as many merchants adopt the plan of posting *only* from the Day Book, and as there are some very good reasons for adopting this policy, we have here given it practical endorsement. The initials, "D. B.," "C. B.," and "B. B.," in the margin of the Sales Book, (standing for Day Book, Cash Book, and Bill Book) will indicate the books wherein are entered the various resources received for merchandise. The Sales Book is not, properly speaking, a book of *results*, and is not consulted in making up our list of resources and liabilities.

In the former set the result of the business was a gain; in this a loss has been sustained, which is shared equally by the two partners.

In writing up this set the student should be required to observe the order of dates in the various books, and complete the record of each transaction before proceeding to the next. For example: On the 1st of July, Robert Van Schaick purchased of us a bill of merchandise for which he paid cash. This entry is first made in the Sales Book, from which the amount is transferred to the Cash Book, and marked "C. B." in the margin of the Sales Book. The succeeding entries in the Sales Book are, in the same manner, transferred to the appropriate books which are indicated in the margin.

DAY BOOK,—SET III.

Albany, July 1, 1861.

1	*H. B. Bryant, Cr.*		
	For Investment in Business, viz.:		
	Merchandise, as per Inventory,	*$4750*	
	Notes, as per Bill Book,	*1500*	
	Cash, as per Cash Book,	*1200*	
	Balances due on Personal Accounts, viz.:		
	John R. Penn,	*500*	
	L. Fairbanks,	*750*	
	Alonzo Gaston,	*375*	*9075*
	"		
1	*H. D. Stratton, Cr.*		
	For Investment, as follows:		
	House and Lot, valued at	*5000*	
	Cash in Union Bank,	*3000*	*8000*
	"		
1	*John R. Penn, Dr.*		
	To Balance favor of H. B. Bryant,		*500*
	"		
1	*Lorenzo Fairbanks, Dr.*		
	To Balance favor of H. B. Bryant,		*750*
	"		
2	*Alonzo Gaston, Dr.*		
	To Balance favor of H. B. Bryant,		*375*

DAY BOOK,—SET III.

Albany, July 2, 1861.

Fol.	Entry	Dollars	Cents
1	*John R. Penn,* Cr.		
	By Cash on %,	250	
	3		
2	*James Johnson,* Dr.		
	To Bill of Mdse. per Sales Book,	192	
	5		
2	*Claflin, Mellen & Co., (N. Y.)* Cr.		
	By Invoice Boots and Shoes,	575	
	"		
2	*A. T. Stewart & Co.,* Cr.		
	By Invoice Dry Goods,	757	
	7		
3	*E. B. Rice,* Dr.		
	To Bill of Mdse. per Sales Book,	42	45
	"		
2	*Alonzo Gaston,* Cr.		
	By Cash in full of %,	375	
	10		
3	*Benjamin Payn,* Dr.		
	To Bill of Mdse. per Sales Book,	23	41
	"		
2	*A. T. Stewart & Co.,* Dr.		
	To Cash on %,	300	

Albany, July 12, 1861.

1	H. D. Stratton, Dr.		
	To Accepted Draft, favor of P. R. Spencer, as per Bill Book,	75	
	13		
3	Amos Dean, Dr.		
	To Bill of Mdse. per Sales Book,	180	
	15		
2	Claflin, Mellen & Co., Dr.		
	To Note @ 60 ds., to Balance %,	575	
	〃		
1	H. B. Bryant, Dr.		
	To Cash on Private %,	75	
	16		
1	Lorenzo Fairbanks, Cr.		
	By Cash on %,	350	
	20		
3	Victor M. Rice, Dr.		
	To Bill of Mdse. per Sales Book,	82	88
	Cr.		
3	By Cash on %,	30	
	21		
3	Amos Dean, Cr.		
	By Cash on %,	50	
	23		
3	James Shelden, Dr.		
	To Bill of Mdse. per Sales Book,	132	24

DAY BOOK,—SET III.

Albany, July 24, 1861.

3	E. B. Rice, Cr.		
	By Cash in full of %,	42	45
	25		
4	William Shepard, Dr.		
	To Bill of Mdse. per Sales Book,	37	55
	26		
4	John Belden, Dr.		
	To Bill of Mdse. per Sales Book,	216	50
	"		
2	A. T. Stewart & Co., Dr.		
	To Cash in full of %,	457	
	29		
1	John R. Penn, Cr.		
	By Cash in full of %,	250	
	31		
4	Chas. M. Seeley, Dr.		
	To Mdse. as per Sales Book,	182	40
	Cr.		
4	By Cash on %,	75	

INDEX TO LEDGER,—SET III.

LEDGER,—SET III.

1

Dr. H. B. Bryant. Cr.

1861 July	15	To Cash,	3	75	1861 July	1	By Invest't	1	9075

Dr. H. D. Stratton. Cr.

1861 July	12	To Acceptance	3	75	1861 July	1	By Invest't	1	8000

Dr. John R. Penn. Cr.

1861 July	1	Bal. H.B.B.	1	500	1861 July	2	By Cash,	2	250
						29	" "	4	250
				500	"				500

Dr. Lorenzo Fairbanks. Cr.

1861 July	1	Bal. H.B.B.	1	750	1861 July	16	By Cash,	3	350

LEDGER,—SET III.

Dr. Alonzo Gaston. Cr.

1861 July	1	Bal. H. B. B.	1	375		1861 July	7	By Cash,		375	

Dr. James Johnson. Cr.

1861 July	3	To Mdse.,	2	192							

Dr. Claflin, Mellen & Co. Cr.

1861 July	15	To note @ 60 ds.	3	575		1861 July	5	By Mdse.,	2	575	

Dr. A. T. Stewart & Co. Cr.

1861 July	10	To Cash,	2	300		1861 July	5	By Mdse.,	2	757	
"	26	" "	4	457							
				757						757	

LEDGER,—SET III.

3

Dr. E. B. Rice. Cr.

1861 July	7	To Mdse.,	2	42	45	1861 July	24	By Cash,	4	42	45

Dr. Benjamin Payn. Cr.

1861 July	10	To Mdse.,	2	23	41						

Dr. Amos Dean. Cr.

1861 July	13	To Mdse.,	3	180		1861 July	21	By Cash,	3	50	

Dr. Victor M. Rice. Cr.

1861 July	20	To Mdse.,	3	82	88	1861 July	20	By Cash,		30	

Dr. James Sheldon. Cr.

				$	¢					$	¢
1861 July	23	To Mdse.,	3	132	24						

Dr. William Shepard. Cr.

				$	¢					$	¢
1861 July	25	To Mdse.,	4	37	55						

Dr. John Belden. Cr.

				$	¢					$	¢
1861 July	26	To Mdse.,	4	216	50						

Dr. Charles A. Seeley. Cr.

				$	¢					$	¢
1861 July	31	To Mdse.,	4	182	40	1861 July	31	By Cash,	4	75	

SALES BOOK,—SET III.

1

Albany, July 1, 1861.

C. B.	**Robert Van Schaick,** *Cash.*			
	110 Yds. Merrimack Prints,	@ 11¢	$12 10	
	75 ,, Union ,,	,, 10¢	7 50	
	120 ,, Orange ,,	,, 9½¢	11 40	
	80 ,, Lowell ,,	,, 10¢	8 00	39 00

— 3 —

D. B.	**James Johnson,** *On %.*			
	2 Cases Men's Thick Boots, 24 pr.,	@ $2,	$48 00	
	3 ,, Calf Welt ,, 36 ,,	,, 3,	108 00	
	1 ,, Boys Grain D.S. ,, 12 ,,	,, 3,	36 00	192

— 4 —

B. B.	**E. H. Bender,** *Note @ 60 ds.*			
	1 Case Pemb'n Rem'ts, 1200 Yds.	@ 5½¢	$66 00	
	9 Pieces Lynn Cottons, 270 ,,	,, 11¢	29 70	
	3 ,, Scotch P. Ging. 125 ,,	,, 10¢	12 50	108 20

— 7 —

D. B.	**E. B. Rice,** *On %.*			
	2 Pieces Eagle Cottons, 80 Yds.,	@ 12¢	$9 60	
	3 ,, Garibaldi Twills, 95 ,,	,, 9¢	8 55	
	2 ,, Bl'ch Drills, 90 ,,	,, 11¢	9 90	
	4 ,, Marietta Cloth, 120 ,,	,, 12¢	14 40	42 45

— 8 —

C. B.	**W. H. Clark,** *Cash.*			
	3 Pieces Bar Muslin, 54 Yds.,	@ 13¢	$7 02	
	2 ,, Brilliante, 64 ,,	,, 20¢	12 80	19 82

SALES BOOK,—SET III.

Albany, July 10, 1861.

D.B.	*Benjamin Payn,* On %.			
	6 Pieces Paper Cambric, 72 Yds., @ 8¢	$5 76		
	1 ,, 6-4 Cot. Dam., 36 ,, ,, 40¢	14 40		
	1 ,, Canvas, 25 ,, ,, 13¢	3 25	23	41
	12			
B.B.	*Calvin S. Sill, (Troy,)* Note @ 90 ds.			
	10 Pieces Fancy Linens, 120 Yds., @ 25¢	$30 00		
	20 ,, Crash, Linen, 200 ,, ,, 9¢	18 00		
	15 ,, Eng'h Prints, 200 ,, ,, 22¢	44 00		
	3 Doz. Balmoral Skirts, 36 @ $2 25	81 00	173	
	13			
D.B.	*Amos Dean,* On %.			
	3 Cases Kip Brogans, 72 pr. @ $1 50	$108 00		
	2 ,, Ladies' Sand. 120 ,, ,, 60¢	72 00	180	
	18			
C.B.	*Geo. H. Doty, (Schenectady,)* Cash.			
	2 Cas. Wom. Walk. Shoes, 120 pr. @ $1 00	$120 00		
	1 ,, Lad. Mor. ,, 48 ,, ,, 1 50	72 00		
	4 Pcs. Check Marseilles, 40 Yds. ,, 75¢	30 00		
	10 ,, Cam. Curt. Clh, 120 ,, ,, 25¢	30 00	252	
	20			
D.B.	*Victor M. Rice,* On %.			
	1 Doz. Silk Scarfs, 12 @ 88¢	$10 56		
	4 Pcs. English Tweed, 36 Yds., ,, $1 12	40 32		
	2 ,, Span. Ch. P'ts, 80 ,, ,, 40¢	32 00	82	88

SALES BOOK,—SET III.

Albany, July 22, 1861.

B. B.	*James R. Morgan, (Buf.) Note @ 6 mos.*		
	3 Doz. Elastic Hoop Skirts, 36 @ $2 50 $90 00		
	1 ,, Stella Shawls, 12 ,, 2 00 24 00		
	6 Pcs. Parametta, 300 Yds., ,, 75¢ 225 00	339	
	23		
D. B.	*James Shelden, (Schoharie,) On %.*		
	3 Cases Congress Gaiters, 36 Pr. @ $1 30 $46 80		
	4 ,, Jenny Lind ,, 48 ,, 1 12 53 76		
	2 ,, Misses Sandals, 96 ,, 33¢ 31 68	132	24
	,,		
C. B.	*Robert Metcalf, Cash.*		
	4 Cases Men's Thick Boots, 48 pr. @ $1 50 $72 00		
	3 ,, Calf Welt ,, 36 ,, ,, 2 00 72 00		
	1 ,, Patent Leath. ,, 12 ,, ,, 5 00 60 00		
	1 ,, Misses School Shoes, 60 ,, ,, 50¢ 30 00	234	
	24		
C. B.	*Charles Heydon, (Greenbush,) Cash.*		
	1 Piece Blk. Doeskin, 20 Yds., @ $1 25 $25 00		
	3 Pcs. Corset Jeans, 90 ,, ,, 10¢ 9 00		
	6 ,, De Laine, 180 ,, ,, 40¢ 72 00	106	
	25		
D. B.	*William Shepard, (Hudson,) On %.*		
	6 Pcs. Lancas. Gingham, 250 Yds. @ 10¢ $25 00		
	1 ,, Canvas, 30 ,, ,, 12½¢ 3 75		
	1 ,, Padding, 40 ,, ,, 10¢ 4 00		
	3 ,, Wiggin, 60 ,, ,, 8¢ 4 80	37	55

SALES BOOK,—SET III.

4

Albany, July 25, 1861.

	Rob't Dawes, (Pittsfield, Ms.)	*Cash.*		
C. B.	4 Cases Misses' Fancy Ties, 96 pr. @ 70¢	$67 20		
	2 ,, Ankle Boots, 48 pr. @ $1 25	60 00		
	1 ,, Kid Gaiters, 24 ,, ,, 1 50	36 00	163	20
	— 26 —			
	John Belden, (Utica,)	*On %.*		
D. B.	2 Pcs. Fancy Cassimeres, 50 Yds. @ $1 25	$62 50		
	3 ,, Saco ,, 60 ,, ,, 1 00	60 00		
	9 ,, Hard Times ,, 270 ,, ,, 20¢	54 00		
	2 ,, Striped Satinet, 80 ,, ,, 50¢	40 00	216	50
	— 27 —			
	James H. Lausley,	*Cash.*		
C. B.	1 Doz. Stella Shawls, 12 @ $2 00	$24 00		
	3 ,, Balmoral Skirts, 36 ,, 2 25	81 00		
	2 ,, Silk Scarfs, 24 ,, 88¢	21 12		
	3 ,, Gents. L. Hdkfs., 36 ,, 35¢	12 60	138	72
	— 29 —			
	Wm. H. Fiquet, (Marion, Ala.)	*Cash.*		
C. B.	8 Pcs. Turkey Red Prints, 200 Yds. @ 16¢	$32 00		
	10 ,, English Tweed, 90 ,, ,, 1 00	90 00		
	2 ,, Spanish Check, 80 ,, ,, 40¢	32 00	154	
	— 31 —			
	Charles H. Seeley, (Rochester,)	*On %.*		
D. B.	4 Cas. Miss. Renfrew Boots, 96 pr. @ $1 00	$96 00		
	2 ,, Ladies' Rarey ,, 24 ,, ,, 2 00	48 00		
	2 ,, Miss. Union Gait., 48 ,, ,, 80¢	38 40	182	40

CASH BOOK,–

Cash, Dr.

1861						
July	1	Am't Invested by H. B. Bryant,	1200			
	,,	,, ,, H. D. Stratton, (in bank)	3000			
	,,	Rec'd for Mdse. sold Rob't Van Schaick,	39			
	2	,, on % of I. R. Penn,	250			
	3	,, for Petty Sales,	17	50		
	7	,, of Alonzo Gaston, in full of %,	375			
	8	,, ,, W. H. Clark for Mdse. per S. B.	19	82		
	10	,, Amount of Rob't Bruce's Note,	500			
	12	,, for Petty Sales,	33	50		
	16	,, of Lorenzo Fairbanks, on %,	350			
	18	,, ,, G. H. Doty for Mdse. per S. B.	252		6036	82
					6036	82
	18	Balance on hand,			5403	57
	20	Rec'd on % of Victor M. Rice,	30			
	21	,, ,, Amos Dean,	50			
	23	,, of R. Metcalf for Mdse. per S. B.	234			
	24	,, ,, Cha's Heydon ,, ,, ,,	106			
	,,	,, ,, E. B. Rice in full of %,	42	45		
	25	,, ,, Rob't Dawes,	163	20		
	27	,, ,, I. H. Lausley for Mdse. per S. B.	138	72		
	29	,, ,, W. H. Fiquet ,, ,,	154			
	,,	,, ,, John R. Penn in full of %,	250			
	31	,, ,, Cha's. A. Seeley on %,	75		1243	37
					6646	94
		Balance on hand,			5881	94

SET III.

Cash, Cr.

Date		Particulars	$	cts	$	cts
1861						
July	1	Paid for Postage Stamps and Pens,	5			
	2	,, ,, Printing Hand Bills,	10			
	4	,, C. Jones for Repair. Store, (per ck.)	175			
	5	,, Freight on Mdse., (per ck.)	27	50		
	7	,, Clerk Hire,	25			
	8	,, Expenses to New York,	15	75		
	10	,, A. T. Stewart & Co. on a/c,	300			
	15	,, H. B. Bryant on Private a/c,	75		633	25
		Balance on hand,			5403	57
					6036	82
	19	Paid for Advtst. in Eve. Journal,	15			
	20	,, ,, Petty Expenses,	10			
	21	,, Bill for Carpenter Work, (per ck.)	175			
	,,	,, Drayage, $5; Postage, $3,	8			
	25	,, Clerk Hire,	25			
	,,	,, for Accept. fav. of H. D. Stratton	75			
	26	,, A. T. Stewart in full of a/c,	457		765	
		Balance on hand,			5881	94
					6646	94

BILL BOOK,—SET III.

Receivable.

No.	When Rec'd.	For what Rec'd.	Drawer or Endorser.	Drawee or Maker.	Date.	Term.	When Due.	Amount.		When and How Disposed of.	
	1861				1861		1861			1861	
1	July 1	Invest. H. B. B.	Henry Ivison,	Robert Bruce,	June 7	30 ds.	July 10	500		July 10	Paid.
2	,, 1	,, ,,	Jas. W. Lusk,	S. S. Packard,	Jan. 10	8 mos.	Sep. 13	1000			
3	,, 4	Mdse.,	I. T. Calkins,	E. H. Bender,	July 4	60 ds.	,, 5	108	20		
4	,, 12	,,	G. V. S. Quackenb'h,	Calvin S. Sill,	,, 12	90 ds.	Oct. 13	173			
							1862				
5	,, 22	,,	W. P. Spencer,	James R. Morgan,	,, 22	6 mos.	Jan. 25	339			

Payable.

No.	When Issued.	For what Issued.	Drawer or Endorser.	Drawee or Maker.	Date.	Term.	When Due.	Amount.		When and How Disposed of.	
	1861				1861		1861				
1	July 12	H. D. S.	P. R. Spencer,	H. D. Stratton,	July 12	10 ds.	July 25	75		July 25	Paid.
2	,, 15	To close a/c,	Claflin, Mellen & Co.	Bryant & Stratton,	,, 15	60 ,,	Sep. 16	575			

STATEMENT

SHOWING THE CONDITION OF BUSINESS AT THE CLOSE OF SET III.

Resources.	Dr.		Cr.		Balance.	
1. *From Ledger Accounts.*						
Lorenzo Fairbanks.................	750		350		400	
James Johnson...................	192				192	
Benjamin Payn...................	23	41			23	41
Amos Dean.......................	180		50		130	
Victor M. Rice..................	82	88	30		52	88
James Sheldon...................	132	24			132	24
William Shepard.................	37	55			37	55
John Belden.....................	216	50			216	50
Chas. A. Seeley.................	182	40	75		107	40
2. *From Cash Book.*—Balance of Cash on hand,.................					5881	94
3. *From Bill Book.*						
S. S. Packard's Note, due Sept. 13.................			$1000	00		
E. H. Bender's, " " " 5.................			108	20		
Calvin S. Sill's, " " Oct. 13.................			173	00		
Jas. R. Morgan's, " " Jan. 25.................			339	00	1620	20
4. *From Inventory.*						
Merchandise unsold.......................................					3000	
Real Estate..					5000	
					16794	12
Liabilities.						
From Bill Book.—Note favor Clafflin, Mellen & Co................					575	
PRESENT WORTH..................................					16219	12

To ascertain the net loss of the concern, and the present worth of each partner, we have the following facts:

H. B. Bryant invested............................	$9075	
" drew out	75	
Net Investment,.....................		$9000
H. D. Stratton invested...........................	$8000	
" drew out..........................	75	
Net Investment....................		7925
Total Net Investment..............		$16925
Deduct Present Worth..............		16219 12
Leaves NET LOSS..................		$705 88
H. B. Bryant's Net Investment....................	$9000	
Less ½ Net Loss............................	352 94	
Leaves Present Worth.......................		8647 06
H. D. Stratton's Net Investment..................	$7925	
Less ½ Net Loss............................	352 94	
Leaves Present Worth.......................		7572 06
TOTAL PRESENT WORTH..............		$16219 12

From the foregoing statement we deduce the following

RULES.

1. *To ascertain the* NET LOSS *during business, subtract the net capital at closing from the net capital at commencing.*
2. *To ascertain the* NET CAPITAL *of each partner at closing, subtract his* NET LOSS *from, or add his* NET GAIN *to his* NET INVESTMENT.

EXAMPLES FOR PRACTICE.

EXAMPLE I.—A. commenced business with a cash capital of $8750. At the close of the year his resources and liabilities were as follows: Cash on hand, $3700; Notes on hand, $7000; Merchandise unsold, $2500; Amounts owing on Personal Accounts, $2000;—He owes on notes, $5000; To various persons, $2500. *What has been his loss? What is his net capital at closing?*

EXAMPLE II.—E. and F. enter into copartnership on equal terms, each investing at commencement, $10,000; and each withdrawing during the business, $1500. At the close of a certain period the following exhibit shows the true condition of their affairs: Cash on hand, $500; Balance in Bank, $7000; Due them on Personal Accounts, $5783 75, of which $875 is worthless; Due them on Notes, $6750; Merchandise on hand, $2700; Real Estate, $5000; Bank Stock, $3500; They owe to persons on account, $10,000; On Notes, $5600. *Have they gained or lost in business, and how much? What is each partner's net capital at closing?*

EXAMPLE III.—A. B. and C. are partners. A. puts into the concern, $7500; B., $5300; C., $4700. At the close of the year their books exhibit the following results: John Smith, Dr. $1700, Cr. $500; John Parker, Dr. $1100, Cr. $975; Abram Schenck, Dr. $1750, Cr. $2700; Albert Dodge, Dr., $1859 38, Cr. $212 50; Cash received, $125,368 29; Paid out, $122,480 23; Notes received, $1900; Notes disposed of, $1200; Merchandise unsold, $2700; Value of Store and Fixtures, $15,750; A. has drawn out $2000; B., $1500; C., $785; They have issued Notes to the amount of $30,000, of which they have redeemed $25,800. *Required a written statement which shall exhibit all these facts, as also, the amount of gain or loss during the business, and each partner's net capital at closing.*

EXERCISES FOR THE LEARNER.

THIRD SERIES.

Memoranda.

July 1. S. S. Packard and John R. Penn commence business with the following resources and liabilities; gains and losses to be divided equally. S. S. Packard invests *Cash*, $4000; *Merchandise*, $1750; *Notes*, as follows: one for $500, in favor of S. S. P., signed by H. B. Bryant, and endorsed by W. P. Spencer, dated June 1, @ 60 ds.; and one for $700, an accepted draft, drawn by L. S. Bliss on George Claghorn, May 1, at 90 ds. sight, and accepted May 3; *Personal Accounts*, as follows: Henry Fish, $500; Robert Fulton, $750; David Coleman, $900. John R. Penn invests, *Cash*, $500; *Real Estate*, $5000.—**2.** Sold N. Frederick, on %, 2 Doz. Gent's Silk Handkerchiefs, 24, @ 40¢; 6 Pcs. Amoskeag Sheeting, 130 Yds., @ 10¢; 4 do. Mixed Cassimeres, 100 Yds., @ 50¢.—Rec'd Cash of Henry Fish, in full of %, $500.—Paid Cash for Stationery and Printing, $30.—**3.** Sold Ira Packard on his acceptance, at 10 days, 1 Case Child's Metallic Tip Shoes, 60 Prs., @ 50¢; 2 do. Child's Heel Gaiters, 96 Prs., @ 63¢; 3 Pcs. English Tweed, 27 Yds., @ $1.—**4.** Sold Wm. T. Bush, on %, 4 Cases Men's Congress Gaiters, 96 Prs., @ $1 50; 2 do. Gent's Canada Ties, 24 Prs., @ $1 75.—Sold James Magoon, for Cash, 1 Piece Striped Velvet, 10 Yds., @ $5; 6 do. Paper Cambrics, 72 Yds., @ 8¢; 10 do. Lynn Cottons, 300 Yds., at 11¢.—**5.** Paid Cash for petty Expenses, $3 75. —Sold Robert Smith, on his note at 60 days, 3 Pcs. Lancaster Gingham, 125 Yds., @ 10¢; 6 do. Scotch Plaid, 240 Yds., @ 13¢.—Bought of Star, Barnum & Seeley, Invoice of Merchandise, amounting to $5000; Paid Cash, $2500; Note, at 6 months, $2500.—**6.** Rec'd Cash on % of David Coleman, $500.—Sold Roger Williams, for Cash, 1 Case Misses Cork Sole Shoes, 60 Prs., @ 75¢; 1 do. Gent's Paris Gaiters, 24 Prs., @ $1 75.—Rec'd Cash for petty Sales, $25 50.—**7.** Sold John Fitch, on %, 3 Doz. Elastic Hoop Skirts, 36, @ $2 50; 1 Doz. "Empress" do., 12, @ $2; 3 Pcs. Check Marseilles, 30 Yds., @ 50¢.—Sold Samuel Nash, for Cash, 3 Pcs. English Tweed, 27 Yds., @ $1; 6 do. Corduroy, 250 Yds., @ 75¢.—Rec'd Cash of Wm. T. Bush, on %, $50.—**9.** Paid John R. Penn, Cash on private %, $100.—Paid Cash for petty Expenses, $7 50.—**10.**

Sold John Anderson, for Cash, 3 Cases Ladies' Extra Balmoral Boots, 144 Prs., @ $2; 2 Cases Ladies' "Opera" Gaiters, 48, @ $1 75.—**12.** Paid S. S. Packard, Cash on private %, $75.—Sold Thomas Hunter, on %, 6 Pcs. Merrimack Prints, 210 Yds., @ 9¢; 5 do. "Union" Prints, 150 Yds., @ 8¢; 7 do. Lancaster Prints, 244 Yds., @ 8½¢; 4 do. Orange Prints, 120 Yds., @ 8½¢.—Rec'd Cash for petty Sales, $10 38.—**13.** Rec'd Cash of David Coleman, in full of %, $400.—Sold John Howard, on %, 3 Pcs. Lancaster Gingham, 125 Yds., @ 10¢; 2 do. French Merino, 40 Yds., @ 50¢; 5 do. Bar. Muslin, 90 Yds., @ 14¢.—**14.** Sold Robert Coons, for Cash, 6 Pcs. Fancy Linens, 36 Yds., @ $2; 5 do. English Prints, 200 Yds., @ 20¢; 6 do. Parametta (Maroon), 300 Yds., @ 75¢.—Paid Cash for Repairing Store, $75.—**16.** Rec'd Cash of John Fitch, in full of %, $129.—Sold Henry Fish, on %, 5 Pcs. Amoskeag Stripes, 120 Yds., @ 12½¢; 4 do. Pepperell Sheeting, 160 Yds., @ 10¢; 4 do. Auburn Sheeting, 120 Yds., @ 15¢.—**17.** Rec'd Cash in full of Robert Fulton's %, $750.—Sold Simon Walker, on his note at 60 days, 4 Cases Men's Thick Boots, 48 Prs., @ $1 25; 2 do. Double-Soled Boots, 24 Prs., @ $1 50.—**20.** Sold Geo. F. Smith, for Cash, 2 Cases Women's Walking Shoes, 120 Prs., @ 50¢; 2 do. Jenny Lind Gaiters, 24 Prs., @ $1 15; 2 do. "Opera" Gaiters, 24 Prs., @ $1 75. —Paid Clerk hire in Cash, $65.—**21.** Rec'd Cash of Henry Fish, in full of %, $49.

STATEMENT

OF RESOURCES AND LIABILITIES, July 21.

The student should be required to make his books conform to the following statement, and to render the same, according to the Example given in connection with Set III.

Resources.			Liabilities.		
Personal Accounts......	$315	54	Notes, payable........	$2500	
Notes, receivable........	1457	18	S. S. P.'s Net Investment	9025	
Cash..................	5286	49	J. R. P.'s.............	5400	
Merchandise (per Inv.)...	4500				
Real Estate............	5000				
Net Loss..........	365	79			
	$16925	00		$16925	00

SET IV.

FURNITURE AND CABINET BUSINESS.

(TWO PARTNERS, ADMITTING A THIRD.)

DAY BOOK, SALES BOOK, LEDGER, CASH BOOK, AND TIME BOOK.

WITH AN IMPROVED METHOD OF USING THE SALES BOOK AS A PRINCIPAL BOOK, AND EMBRACING VALUABLE INSTRUCTIONS PERTAINING TO A CHANGE IN BUSINESS.

Business Prosperous.

REMARKS.

It is intended in this Set to realize, as nearly as may be, the capabilities of Single Entry. With this view we have introduced several new features, to which we call special attention.

It has been the pleasure of certain authors and teachers to condemn Single Entry Book-keeping as wholly inadequate to the demands of business, and, therefore, unworthy of consideration; but while we are behind no one in our admiration of the superior facilities and safeguards of Double Entry, we are not at all prepared to conclude that a very extensive business may not be conducted with perfect safety, having no better record than that afforded by an intelligent and faithful application of the principles of Single Entry Book-keeping. This fact, together with another of equal force, viz., that in many of the first-class houses in our large commercial cities, Single Entry is preferred, affords sufficient cause for attempting to present its strongest points to the public.

The materials from which the transactions in this Set are constructed, were obtained from an extensive cabinet warehouse in New York, and the routine has the merit, at least, of being business-like. The forms of the books, and arrangement of the various records, are submitted as the most simple and practical in use.

One important feature in this Set is the use of the Sales Book distinct from the Day Book. In Set III, although a Sales Book is used, all sales *on credit* are first transferred to the Day Book, and from thence posted into the Ledger. Here, however, the credit sales are posted to the personal accounts *directly from the Sales Book*. This affords a great saving of time, and is, in all respects, quite as satisfactory. The figures in the margin of the Sales Book refer to the Ledger page to which the amounts are posted; the initials "C. B." and "B. B." indicate that the result of the sales thus marked, are shown in the Cash Book and Bill Book. The former of these is exhibited at length; the latter has been omitted, although it is expected that the learner will supply it, after the form given in Set III.

REMARKS.

The taking in of a new partner forms another important feature of this Set, and one which will afford the learner some of the most valuable hints connected with Accounts. It is a settled principle in Accounts, or should be, that whenever any change in the business occurs, the existing resources and liabilities of the concern should be made apparent; and, consequently, the proprietors' accounts should represent their net investment *at the time of the change*. The same rule holds good respecting the landmarks of business, or the financial eras, such as the close of a fiscal year, or any important event which makes it necessary to exhibit on the main books the exact condition of the business.

In the case under consideration, the existing partners, "Lester and Brown," propose to admit a new partner, who shall invest equally with them, and share equally in the gains and losses. The partners' accounts now show only their *original* investment; and it will be evident that, if the new partner invests an amount just equal to this, he will unjustly become a joint-partner in the gains which have already accrued, but which remain unacknowledged in the business. The original partners, it is plain, are entitled to all the avails of the concern previous to admitting the new partner, and if their own proper accounts do not show what this net amount is, they should be made to. Therefore, before deciding how much the new partner should invest to place him on an equal footing with his associates, it becomes necessary to credit the original partners with their respective gains during business. With this view the statement on the third page of the Day Book is made, and the partners thereafter credited, each with his net gain. The partners' accounts in the Ledger are then closed up, and the balances brought down as a new capital, which is, of course, the amount that the new partner must invest.

The general Statement which follows this Set affords, perhaps, as convenient a form for such statements as any in use. The student cannot too carefully study the philosophy of these, nor be too particular in drawing them up, as to their neatness and perspicuity. An obscure or insufficient statement of a business, however prosperous and satisfactory may be the condition which it aims to show, is like a good story so bunglingly told that its chief points are obscured, and its moral entirely lost sight of.

For simplicity, directness, and efficiency, the forms and general plan of Set IV are submitted as a model.

DAY BOOK,—SET IV.

Brooklyn, April 1, 1861.

	James Lester and Robert Brown enter into Copartnership this day, as Dealers in Furniture and Cabinet-ware, under the firm-title of "Lester & Brown;" Mr. Lester transferring to the firm the Assets and Liabilities of a former Business, and Mr. Brown investing an equivalent in Cash, as per terms of Contract.		
1	James Lester, — Cr. By Investment, as follows: Mdse., (finished articles,) per I. B., $3000 00 Materials and Unfinished Work, ,, 2500 00 Tools and Implements, 300 00 Notes on hand, per Bill Book, 1375 00 Balance of David Owens' %, 230 00 ,, ,, Thomas Webster's %, 57 30 ,, ,, Timothy Paywell's %, 175 00	7637	30
1	James Lester, — Dr. To the following Debts, assumed by Firm: Note favor Joseph Wiggins, due Ap. 20, $500 00 ,, ,, Peter Jones, ,, Sep. 10, 250 00 Balance due Austin Packard on %, 175 00 ,, ,, I. W. Bulkley, ,, 230 00	1155	
	,,		
1	Robert Brown, — Cr. By Cash,	6482	30
	,,		
1	David Owens, — Dr. To Balance due I. L.,	230	
	,,		
1	Thomas Webster, — Dr. To Balance due I. L.,	57	30

DAY BOOK,—SET IV.

2

Brooklyn, April 1, 1861.

2	*Timothy Paywell,* *Dr.*		
	To Balance due I. L.,	175	
	"		
2	*Austin Packard,* *Cr.*		
	By Balance due from I. L.,	175	
	"		
2	*I. W. Bulkley,* *Cr.*		
	By Balance due from I. L.,	230	
	2		
1	*David Owens,* *Cr.*		
	By Cash to Bal. %,	230	
	4		
3	*H. W. Clark,* *Cr.*		
	By Cash on %,	50	
	15		
1	*Thomas Webster,* *Cr.*		
	By Cash in full of %,	57	30
	18		
2	*Austin Packard,* *Dr.*		
	To Cash in full of %,	175	
	20		
3	*Richard Bannister,* *Cr.*		
	By Cash on %,	30	
	25		
3	*Roger Bacon,* *Cr.*		
	By Cash in full of %,	43	50

Brooklyn, April 27, 1861.

Richard Bannister, Cr.			
By Note @ 30 ds., to Balance %,		37	

——NEW FIRM.——

May 1

Messrs. Lester & Brown have this day associated with them, Robert Lincoln, who is to invest an equal amount of Capital, and share equally in Gains and Losses, as per Contract. The Books of "Lester & Brown" are therefore made to exhibit their Resources and Liabilities, each partner being credited with his share of the Net Gain, and the Balances brought down as a New Investment. The new firm is to be styled "Lester, Brown & Co."

Following is an exhibit of Lester & Brown's affairs:

Resources.			
Bal. due on personal acc'ts, per Ledger,	$416 00		
Cash on hand, per Cash Book,	6374 38		
Notes ,, ,, Bill Book,	1016 50		
Value of Finished Stock, per Inven'y,	3500 00		
,, Unfinished ,, ,, ,,	1875 00		
,, Tools and Implements,	500 00	13681	88
Liabilities.			
Bal. due on personal acc'ts, per Ledger,		175	
Present Worth,		13506	88
James Lester's Investment,	6482 30		
Robert Brown's ,,	6482 30	12964	60
Net Gain,		542	28
James Lester's ½ net gain, $271 14			
Robert Brown's ½ ,, ,, 271 14	542 28		

DAY BOOK,—SET IV.

Brooklyn, May 1, 1861.

1	James Lester,	Cr.		
	By Net Gain, per Statement,		271	14
	"			
1	Robert Brown,	Cr.		
	By Net Gain, per Statement,		271	14
	"			
4	Robert Lincoln,	Cr.		
	By Cash Invested,		6753	44
	"			
4	Central Bank,	Dr.		
	To Cash Deposited,		12000	
	5			
3	John Anderson,	Cr.		
	By Cash in full of %,		65	
	8			
2	Timothy Paywell,	Cr.		
	By Cash in full of %,		175	
	9			
2	J. W. Bulkley,	Dr.		
	To Cash in full of %,		121	
	31			
1	James Lester,	Cr.		
	By Net Gain, per Statement,		187	73
	"			
1	Robert Brown,	Cr.		
	By Net Gain, per Statement,		187	73
	"			
4	Robert Lincoln,	Cr.		
	By Net Gain, per Statement,		187	74

SALES BOOK,—SET IV.

1

Brooklyn, April 2, 1861.

	H. H. Low, *Brooklyn.*			
2	*1 Rosewood Tete-a-tete,*	*$60 00*		
	1 Gothic Mahogany Bedstead,	*20 00*		
	6 Mahogany Chairs, Carved,	*25 00*		
	1 Marble-Top Table,	*15 00*	*120*	
	Chgd. to %.			
	,,			
	H. W. Beecher, *Brooklyn,*			
C. B.	*1 Dressing Bureau, Serpentine Front,*	*$22 00*		
	1 Lounge for Study,	*15 00*		
	1 Gothic Hall Stand, R. W.,	*24 00*	*61*	
	Recd. Cash.			
	3			
	H. W. Clark, *Williamsburg,*			
3	*6 Cane-bottom Chairs, Mgy.,*	*$15 00*		
	1 Black Walnut Tete-a-Tete,	*25 00*		
	1 Mgy. Centre Table,	*14 00*		
	1 ,, Card Table, O. G. Front,	*7 00*	*61*	
	Chgd. to %.			
	4			
	J. J. Powell, *Jamaica,*			
B. B.	*1 Card Table, Mgy.,*	*$8 00*		
	1 Sofa ,, B. W.,	*9 00*		
	1 Piano Stool, R. W.,	*7 50*		
	2 Small Wash Stands, @ $2 50,	*5 00*	*29*	*50*
	Note @ 30 ds.			
	,,			
	Thomas Proctor, *Yonkers,*			
C. B.	*1 French Bedstead, B. W.,* Recd. Cash.		*15*	

SALES BOOK,—SET IV.

Brooklyn, April 5, 1861.

Fol.				
2	J. W. Bulkley,	Williamsburg,		
	1 Pair Ottomans, B. W.,		$10 00	
	1 Lounge, Brocatelle,		15 00	
	6 Parlor Chairs, R. W.,		30 00	55
		Chgd. to %.		
	6			
C. B.	John N. Pattison,	New York,		
	1 Piano Stool,		$8 00	
	1 Music Rack,		4 00	12
		Rec'd Cash.		
	7			
3	Richard Bannister,	Chester,		
	1 Stuffed-back Chair,		$15 00	
	1 Cottage Bedstead, B. W.,		12 00	
	1 Gothic ,,		20 00	
	4 Parlor Chairs, Mgy.,		16 00	
	1 Corner Stand, ,,		4 00	67
		Chgd. to %.		
	,,			
C. B.	Henry W. Taylor,	Brooklyn,		
	1 Double-Leaf Secretary,		$35 00	
	1 Enameled Cloth Lounge,		10 00	45
		Rec'd Cash.		
	8			
C. B.	T. L. Cuyler,	Brooklyn,		
	1 Extension Dining Table,		$14 00	
	6 Kitchen Chairs,		3 00	
	1 Book Case, R. W.,		40 00	
	1 Hall Stand, ,,		15 00	72
		Rec'd Cash.		

SALES BOOK,—SET IV.

Brooklyn, April 10, 1861.

C. B.	Robert Mc Grath,	Islip,		
	2 Quartette Tables, Mgy.,	$5 00		
	1 Sofa Table, Lyre Front,	11 00		
	1 Large Arm Chair,	12 00		
	2 Sew. Chairs, Cane Bot.,	6 50	34	50
	Recd. Cash.			
	12			
C. B.	James Smith,	Hempstead,		
	12 Dining Chairs, @ $1 50	$18 00		
	1 ,, Table,	15 00	33	
	Recd. Cash.			
	15			
3	Roger Bacon,	Haverstraw,		
	1 Lady's Arm Chair, R. W.,	$10 00		
	1 ,, Sewing ,, ,,	7 50		
	1 Card Table, ,,	6 00		
	1 Cabinet Box, R. W.,	20 00	43	50
	Chgd. to %.			
	18			
C. B.	William F. Turner,	Brooklyn,		
	1 Single Bedstead,	$6 00		
	6 Cottage Chairs, @ $1 75	10 50		
	1 Quartette Table,	5 00	21	50
	Recd. Cash.			
	20			
3	John Anderson,	Brooklyn,		
	1 Set Enam. Furniture, Chgd. to %.		65	
	25			
B. B.	James E. Jenkins,	Brooklyn,		
	1 Sofa Bedstead, Patent,	$45 00		
	6 Parlor Chairs, Broc.,	30 00	75	
	Note @ 60 ds.			

SALES BOOK,—SET IV.

Brooklyn, April 28, 1861.

Folio	Particulars			
	David Woods, *Red Hook,*			
C. B.	1 Tete-a-tete, B. W. and Broc.,	$40 00		
	1 Easy Rocker, ,, ,, ,,	25 00		
	1 Corner Stand,	4 50	69	50
	Recd. Cash.			
	— 30 —			
	H. W. Clark, *Williamsburg,*			
3	1 Sofa Bedstead, Patent, Chgd. to %.		45	
	NEW FIRM.			
	— May 1 —			
	Peter Jamieson, *Morrisania,*			
C. B.	1 "Sleepy Hollow" Chair,	$18 00		
	1 Enameled Bedstead,	20 00		
	1 ,, Wash Stand,	5 00	43	
	Recd. Cash.			
	— 3 —			
	H. H. Low, *Brooklyn,*			
2	2 Gothic Chairs, B. W. Stuffed,	$30 00		
	1 Set Enam. Furniture,	75 00	105	
	Chgd. to %.			
	— 5 —			
	Joseph Brooks, *Bellvale,*			
4	2 Cupboard Washstands, @ $6 00	$12 00		
	1 Hat Rack,	5 00		
	1 Dining Table,	14 00		
	1 Black Walnut Crib,	5 00	36	
	Chgd. to %.			

SALES BOOK,—SET IV.

Brooklyn, May 6, 1861.

Folio	Particulars		Amount	Total
	J. W. Bulkley,	Williamsburg,		
2	1 Centre Table, B. W., Carved,		$25 00	
	1 Bureau, Serpentine Front,		24 50	
	1 Side "What-not,"		4 50	54
		Chgd. to %.		
	10			
	Richard Bannister,	Chester,		
3	1 Reclining Chair, Patent,		$12 50	
	1 High Book Case, B. W.,		40 00	
	1 Pair Footstools,		4 50	57
		Chgd. to %.		
	15			
	C. L. Derby,	New York,		
C. B.	1 Set Enameled Furniture,		$75 00	
	1 Tete-a-Tete,		30 00	
	1 Rosewood Sofa,		60 00	165
		Recd. Cash.		
	18			
	Ivison, Phinney & Co.,	New York,		
C. B.	1 B. W. Lib'y Book Case,	Recd. Cash.		75
	20			
	W. L. Stimson,	Penn Yan,		
C. B.	2 Plain Wash Stands,		$4 00	
	1 French Bedstead, B. W.,		25 00	
	1 Single " "		10 00	
	6 Dining Chairs, @ $1 50,		9 00	
	3 Parlor " " 4 50,		13 50	61 50
		Recd. Cash.		

SALES BOOK,—SET IV.

Brooklyn, May 20, 1861.

Ref.	Particulars			$	cts.
4	Steamer Isaac Newton, North River,				
	6 Rosewood Tete-a-tetes,	@ $35 00	$210 00		
	24 ,, Chairs,	,, 5 00	120 00		
	3 Stufd. Broc. Arm Chairs,	,, 25 00	75 00		
	1 Carved Rosewood Centre Table,		50 00	455	
	Chgd. to %.				
	25				
2	A. M. Low, Brooklyn.				
	150 Orchestra Chairs, for Academy of Music, @ $4 00			600	
	Chgd. to %.				
	28				
C. B.	George McDougal, New York,				
	1 Hall Stand,		$4 00		
	6 Parlor Chairs, @ $2 75		16 50		
	1 Wash Stand,		10 00	30	50
	Recd. Cash.				
	30				
C. B.	Abraham Fuller, Jamaica,				
	1 Black Walnut Sofa,		$30 00		
	1 Tete-a-tete,		25 00		
	1 Large Dining Table,		16 00		
	2 Gothic Chairs,		10 00	81	
	Recd. Cash.				
	,,				
C. B.	R. Van Norman, New York,				
	1 Piano Stool,		$10 00		
	1 Music Rack,		5 00		
	3 Arm-chairs, Rosewood,		45 00	60	
	Recd. Cash.				

LEDGER,—SET IV.

1

Dr. James Lester. Cr.

1861						1861					
Apr.	1	Sund. Debts,	1	1155		Apr.	1	By Invest'd,	1	7637	30
May	1	To Balance,		6753	44	May	1	,, Net Gain	4	271	14
				7908	44					7908	44
May	31	To Balance,		6941	17	May	1	By Balance,		6753	44
						,,	31	,, Net Gain		187	73
				6941	17					6941	17
						June	1	By Balance,		6941	17

Dr. Robert Brown. Cr.

1861						1861					
May	1	To Balance,		6753	44	Apr.	1	By Cash Inv.	1	6482	30
						May	1	,, Net Gain	4	271	14
				6753	44					6753	44
May	31	To Balance,		6941	17	May	1	By Balance,		6753	44
						,,	31	,, Net Gain		187	73
				6941	17					6941	17
						June	1	By Balance,		6941	17

Dr. David Owens. Cr.

1861						1861					
Apr.	1	Bal. due J. L.	1	230		Apr.	2	By Cash,	2	230	

Dr. Thomas Webster. Cr.

1861						1861					
Apr.	1	Bal. due J. L.	1	57	30	Apr.	15	By Cash,	2	57	30

Dr. Timothy Paywell Cr.

1861						1861				
Apr.	1	Bal. due I. L.	2	175		May	8	By Cash,	4	175

Dr. Austin Packard. Cr.

1861						1861				
Apr.	18	To Cash,	2	175		Apr.	1	Bal. from I. L.	1	175

Dr. J. W. Bulkley. Cr.

1861						1861				
Apr.	5	To Sund. S. B.	2	55		Apr.	1	Bal. from I. L.	1	230
,,	30	,, Balance,		175						
				230						230
May	6	To Sund. S. B.	5	54		May	1	By Balance,		175
,,	9	,, Cash,	4	121						
				175						175

Dr. A. A. Low. Cr.

1861						1861				
Apr.	2	To Sund. S. B.	1	120		May	31	By Balance,		825
May	3	,, ,, ,,	4	105						
,,	25	150 Chairs ,,	6	600						
				825						
May	31	To Balance,		825						

Dr. H. W. Clark. Cr.

Date			Fo.	$	cts.	Date			Fo.	$	cts.
1861						1861					
Apr.	3	To Sund. S.B.	1	61		Apr.	4	By Cash,	2	50	
"	30	" " .	4	45		"	30	" Balance,		56	
				106						106	
May	1	To Balance,		56							

Dr. Richard Bannister. Cr.

Date			Fo.	$	cts.	Date			Fo.	$	cts.
1861						1861					
Apr.	7	To Sund. S.B.	2	67		Apr.	20	By Cash,	2	30	
						"	27	" Note,	3	37	
				67						67	
May	10	To Sund. S.B.	5	57							

Dr. Roger Bacon. Cr.

Date			Fo.	$	cts.	Date			Fo.	$	cts.
1861						1861					
Apr.	15	To Sund. S.B.	3	43	50	Apr.	25	By Cash,	2	43	50

Dr. John Anderson. Cr.

Date			Fo.	$	cts.	Date			Fo.	$	cts.
1861						1861					
Apr.	20	To Sund. S.B.	3	65		Apr.	5	By Cash,	4	65	

Dr. Joseph Brooks. Cr.

1861 May	5	To Sund. S. B.	4	36							

Dr. Robert Lincoln. Cr.

1861 May	31	To Balance,		6941	18	1861 May	1	By Cash Inv.	4	6753	44
						,,	31	,, Net Gain,	,,	187	74
				6941	18					6941	18
						June	1	By Balance,		6941	18

Dr. Central Bank. Cr.

1861 May	1	Cash Dep.	4	12000							

Dr. Steamer Isaac Newton. Cr.

1861 May	20	To Sund. S. B.	6	455							

Cash, Dr.

1861						
Apr.	1	Am't Invested, Robert Brown,			6482	30
	2	Rec'd of H. W. Beecher, per S. B.,	61			
	,,	,, ,, David Owens, in full of %,	230			
	4	,, ,, Thomas Proctor, per S. B.,	15			
	,,	,, ,, H. W. Clark, on %,	50			
	6	,, ,, John N. Pattison, per S. B.,	12			
	7	,, ,, Henry W. Taylor, ,, ,,	45			
	,,	,, Am't due on John Simpson's note,	500			
	8	,, of T. L. Cuyler, per S. B.,	72			
	10	,, ,, Robert McGrath,	34	50		
	12	,, ,, James Smith,	33			
	15	,, ,, Thomas Webster, in full of %,	57	30		
	18	,, ,, William Turner, per S. B.,	21	50		
	20	,, ,, Richard Bannister, on %,	30			
	25	,, ,, Roger Bacon, in full of %,	43	50		
	28	,, ,, David Woods, per S. B.,	69		1273	80
					7756	10
		Balance brought down,			6374	38
May	1	Am't Invested by Robert Lincoln,	6753	44		
	,,	Rec'd of Peter Jamieson, per S. B.,	43			
	5	,, ,, John Anderson, in full of %,	65			
	8	,, ,, Timothy Paywell, ,, ,,	175			
	15	,, ,, C. S. Derby, per S. B.,	165			
	18	,, ,, Ivison, Phinney & Co., p. S.B.	75			
	20	,, ,, W. L. Stimson, ,, ,,	61	50		
	28	,, ,, George McDougal, ,, ,,	30	50		
	30	,, ,, Abraham Fuller, ,, ,,	81			
	,,	,, ,, R. VanNorman, ,, ,,	60		7509	44
					13883	82
		Balance brought down,			1003	02

SET IV.

Cash, Cr.

1861						
Apr.	1	Paid for Stat'y, $5; Post. Stamps, $3;	8			
	2	,, I. Stevens & Co. bill Box Lumber,	75			
	,,	,, for Glue and Varnish p. Exp. Book,	18	75		
	4	,, ,, Hair Cloth, per I. White's Bill,	150			
	5	,, ,, Copy. Refs, $6; Let. Book, $2;	8			
	6	,, Workmen Wages to date, p. Time B.,	128	17		
	8	,, Simpson's bill for B. W. Lumber,	350			
	10	,, Petty Expenses, per Expense Book,	15	30		
	13	,, Workmen's Wages, per Time Book,	121	33		
	15	,, Prem. Insur. on Building & Contents	85			
	18	,, Austin Packard in full of %,	175			
	20	,, Workmen's Wages, per Time Book,	113	17		
	25	,, Drayage, $10; Post. Stamps, $3;	13			
	27	,, Workmen's Wages, per Time Book,	121		1381	72
		Balance on hand,			6374	38
					7756	10
May	1	Deposited in Central Bank,	12000			
	3	Paid Sundry Expenses, per Expen. Book,	18	75		
	4	,, Fisher & Bird's bill for Marble,	115			
	,,	,, Workmen's Wages, per Time Book,	117	50		
	9	,, I. W. Bulkley, in full of %,	121			
	11	,, Workmen's Wages, per Time Book,	128	75		
	15	,, Sundry Expenses, per Expen. Book,	24	30		
	18	,, Workmen's Wages, per Time Book,	98	50		
	20	,, L. Johnson's bill for Plush, etc.,	124			
	25	,, Workmen's Wages, per Time Book,	113	75		
	28	,, Sundry Expenses, per Expen. Book,	19	25	12880	80
		Balance on hand,			1003	02
					13883	82

TIME BOOK.—SET IV.

APRIL, 1861.	Wages per Week	Monday	Tuesday	Wednesday	Thursday	Friday	Saturday			Monday.	Tuesday.	Wednesday.	Thursday.	Friday.	Saturday.			Monday.	Tuesday.	Wednesday.	Thursday.	Friday.	Saturday.			Monday.	Tuesday.	Wednesday.	Thursday.	Friday.	Saturday.		
NAMES.		1	2	3	4	5	6	Amt.		8	9	10	11	12	13	Amt.		15	16	17	18	19	20	Amt.		22	23	24	25	26	27	Amt.	
Robert Wood,	20	/	/	/	/	/	/	√20		/	/	/	/	/	/	√20		/	/	/	/	/	/	√20		/	/	/	/	/	/	√20	
Samuel Burns,	15	/	/		/	/	/	√12	50	/	/	/	/	/	/	√15		/	/	/	/	/	/	√15		/	/	/	/	/	/	√15	
P. O'Toole,	10	/	/			/	/	√6	67																								
James Murphy,	10	/	/	/	/	/	/	√10																									
Pat. McGann,	10	/	/	/	/	/	/	√10		/	/	/	/	/	/	√10		/	/	/	/	/	/	√10		/	/					√3	33
John Turk,	10	/	/					√3	33	/	/	/	/	/	/	√10		/	/	/	/	/	/	√10		/	/	/	/			√6	67
Peter Winns,	6	/	/	/	/	/	/	√6		/	/	/	/	/	/	√6		/	/	/	/	/	/	√6		/	/	/	/	/	/	√6	
Abel Jones,	6	/	/	/	/	/	/	√6		/	/	/	/	/	/	√6				/	/	/	/	√4		/	/	/	/	/	/	√6	
A. Jackson,	6	/	/	/	/		/	√5		/	/	/	/	/	/	√6		/	/			/	/	√4		/	/	/	/	/	/	√6	
R. Porter,	6	/	/		/			√3		/	/					√2		/	/	/	/	/	/	√6		/	/	/	/	/	/	√6	
P. Sanford,	6	/	/	/	/	/		√5		/	/	/	/			√4		/	/	/	/	/	/	√6		/	/	/	/	/	/	√6	
F. Molloy,	6		/	/	/	/	/	√5		/	/	/	/			√4		/	/	/	/	/	/	√6		/	/	/	/	/	/	√6	
H. Wait,	6		/	/	/	/	/	√5		/	/	/	/	/	/	√6										/	/	/	/	/	/	√6	
Henry Trim,	6	/	/	/	/	/	/	√6		/	/	/	/	/	/	√6		/	/	/	/	/	/	√6		/	/	/	/	/	/	√6	
P. Bush,	5	/	/	/	/	/	/	√5				/	/	/	/	√3	33		/	/	/	/	/	√4	17	/	/	/	/	/	/	√5	
Aaron Burr,	5	/	/	/	/	/	/	√5		/	/	/	/	/	/	√5		/	/	/	/	/	/	√5		/	/	/	/	/	/	√5	
Thos. Park,	5	/	/	/	/	/	/	√5		/	/	/	/	/	/	√5		/	/	/	/	/	/	√5		/	/	/	/	/	/	√5	
R. Mann,	5		/	/				√1	67	/	/	/	/	/	/	√5										/	/	/	/	/	/	√5	
H. Poore,	5	/	/	/	/	/	/	√5		/	/	/	/	/	/	√5		/	/	/	/	/	/	√5		/	/	/	/	/	/	√5	
S. Parker,	3	/	/	/	/	/	/	√3		/	/	/	/	/	/	√3						/	/	√1		/	/	/	/	/	/	√3	
Total,								128	17							121	33							113	17							121	

STATEMENT

SHOWING THE CONDITION OF THE BUSINESS ON THE 31ST OF MAY.

THE following Statement differs, in no material respect, from those which have preceded it; the only difference being in the form of expressing the gains. There being no debts owing to outside parties, the several amounts due the members of the firm constitute the only liabilities. The sum of these amounts, or the total present worth, must, of course, equal the sum of the resources.

Resources.						
1. *From Ledger Accounts.*—Balances due:						
A. A. Low,			$825			
H. W. Clark			56			
R. Bannister			57			
Joseph Brooks			36			
Central Bank			12000			
Steamer Isaac Newton			455			
2. *From Cash Book.*—Balance of Cash on hand			1003	02		
3. *From Bill Book.*—Notes on hand			1016	50		
4. *From Inventory.*—Valuation of Property:						
Finished Stock on hand			4000			
Unfinished			875			
Tools and Implement			500		$20823	52
Liabilities.						
James Lester's Investment	$6753	44				
" " ⅓ Net Gain	187	73				
" " *Present Worth*			$6941	17		
Robert Brown's Investment	$6753	44				
" " ⅓ Net Gain	187	73				
" " *Present Worth*			6941	17		
Robert Lincoln's Investment	$6753	44				
" " ⅓ Net Gain	187	74				
" " *Present Worth*			6941	18		
TOTAL PRESENT WORTH,					$20823	52

EXAMPLES FOR PRACTICE.

THE principles applied in the foregoing statement have been already sufficiently announced. The examples which follow are intended to afford the student more ample practice in the important labor of expressing financial facts through appropriate forms. Let the solutions be rendered in the form of a Business Statement.

EXAMPLE I.—A and B are equal partners, investing each $10,000. At the end of a year they desire to take C into co-partnership upon condition that he will invest equally with them, and share equally in the results of the business. The following is a statement of their affairs previous to uniting with C: *Personal Accounts*, John Jones, Dr. $1500, Cr. $700; Robert Fulton, Dr. $5000; James Webb, Dr. $1750, Cr. $1000; Clarence Shook, Dr. $5000, Cr. $2500; Lewis Lyman, Cr. $4000; Dr. $3000; W. F. Norman, Cr. $2000; Dr. $1500; *Merchandise unsold*, $7500; *Notes on hand*, $6000; *Notes outstanding*, $2500; *Cash on hand*, $2000. *Required, a statement showing the gain or loss during business, and the net capital of each partner at closing.*

EXAMPLE II.—C and D enter into co-partnership, C to furnish the capital, and D to devote his time to the business—gains and losses to be divided equally. C invests $10,000, and during the year withdraws $2000. D withdraws $1500. At the close of the year, they have: Cash, $3000; Personal accounts, $1500; Merchandise, $10,000; Notes, $1750; they owe, on notes and personal accounts, $5000. *What is the gain or loss in business? What is each partner's capital at closing?*

EXAMPLE III.—J and K enter into co-partnership for the purpose of conducting a Building business; each to receive interest at 7% on his net investment, and the gain or loss to be divided equally. J invests: Materials and Implements, $5000; Unfinished contracts, $6750; Notes, $4800; Personal accounts, $10,000; and the firm assume to pay for him a liability of $1000. K invests: Cash, $10,000; Notes, $15,000. At the close of the year, their books show the following condition: Cash on hand, $15,000; Notes, $5700; Interest on same, $500; Materials and Implements $18,000; Personal accounts, $9400. *What is the net gain or loss? What is each partner's capital at closing?*

EXERCISES FOR THE LEARNER.

FOURTH SERIES.

June 1. William Jones and Thomas Mason, enter into co-partnership. WILLIAM JONES *invests:* Mdse. $4750; Tools and Implements, $750; Notes, $1500; Peter Filkin's %, $500; Robert Hall's do. $700.—THOMAS MASON *invests:* Cash, $8200.—Sold W. D. Packard, on %, 1 set Enameled Furniture, $75; 2 Hair Matrasses, @ $12 each; 1 Mahogany Arm Chair, $15.—**2.** Paid Cash for Stationery, $20.—Sold Robert Banks, for Cash, 1 doz. Dining Chairs, $20; 1 Hall Stand, $8; 1 Mahogany Bedstead, $12. —Paid Cash for Lumber, $25.—Sold George Chrysler, on his note @ 30 ds., 1 Child's Crib, B.W. $6; 1 Mahogany Bureau, $25; 1 Tete-a-tete, R.W. $30.—**3.** Received Cash of Robert Hall, on %, $300.—Sold George A. Crocker, on %, 1 Hall Stand, $6; 2 Light Washstands, 1 @ $5, and 1 @ $7; 12 Kitchen chairs, @ 75¢.—Sold John Hall, for Cash, 1 French Bedstead, $15.—**5.** Paid Workmen, Cash to date, $165.—Sold A. W. Betts, on %, 10 Cane Bottom Chairs, @ $1 75¢ each; 1 Black Walnut Tete-a-tete, $30; 1 Card Table, $10; 3 small Washstands, @ $2 50¢ each.—Sold James Morgan, for Cash, 1 Black Walnut Book-case, $40; 1 Double-leaf Secretary, $30.—**6.** Received Cash for John Jacobs' note, due this day, $500.—Sold Charles Williams, on his note @ 60 ds., 1 Pair Ottomans, $12; 1 Piano Stool, $7; 8 Brocatelle Parlor Chairs, @ $4 each; 1 Sofa Table, $15.—Bo't. of Clark Dunham, on %, 1 Lot Black Walnut Lumber, $900.—**7.** Sold A. W. Betts, on %, 1 Mahogany Centre Table, $15; 1 Cottage Bedstead, $10; 1 Corner Stand, $5.—Sold James W. Lusk, for Cash, 1 Black Walnut Book-case, $50.—Received Cash in full of Peter Filkin's %, $500.—**8.** Sold J. C. Buttre, for Cash, 1 Dressing Bureau, (serpentine front) $25; 1 Study Lounge, $12; 1 Extension Dining Table, $17.—Sold Wm. T. Brooks, on %, 1 Rosewood Tete-a-tete, $50.—**9.** Sold James Moore, for Cash, 1 Quartette Table, $6; 6 Parlor Chairs, @ $5 each; 1 Set Enameled Furniture, $50.—**10.** Paid Cash for Gas Bill, $14 30¢.—Received Cash of A. W. Betts, in full of %, ——.—**12.** Paid Workmen, Cash to date, $275.—Sold Geo. A. Crocker, on %, 6 Parlor Chairs, @ $3; 12 Dining Chairs, @ $1 50; 1 Mantel Clock, $5.—**13.** Sold Benj. F. Butler, on %, 8 doz. Camp Stools, 96 @ 50¢ each; 1 Portable Secretary, $25.—Received Cash on %, of W. D. Packard, $75.—**15.** Sold Robert Hall, on %, 6 Gothic Chairs @ $5 each; 1 French Bedstead, $15; 2 Washstands, @ $4 each.—Sold W. J. Curtiss, for Cash, 1 Book-case, $40; 4 Library Chairs, @ $7 each; 1 Large Rocking Chair, $15.—**17.** Paid Workmen, Cash to date, $218.—Received Cash of Geo. A. Crocker, in full of %, $——.—Sold J. C. Banks, for Cash, 1 Double Bedstead, $10; 1 Single do., $9.—**18.** Paid Clark Dunham, Cash on %, $500. —Sold John Banks, on his note @ 30 ds., 1 Bureau, $30; 1 Sofa Bedstead, $45.—**19.** Sold W. D. Packard, on %, 12 Kitchen Chairs, @ $1 each; 3 Common Bedsteads, @ $5 each; 1 Office Desk, $15. Sold W. T. Brooks, on %, 1 Carved Rosewood Center Table, $45. —**20.** Received Cash of W. D. Packard, in full of %, $——.—**21.** Sold Robert Hall, on %, 1 Teacher's Desk, $25; 12 Dining Chairs, @ $1 75¢; 12 Cane Bottom Settees, @ $8 each.—**22.** Paid Cash, Book-keeper's salary, $75.—Received Cash, in full of William Carter's note, now due, $1000.—**24.** Paid Workmen, Cash to date, $193.—Sold E. A. Charlton, on %, 50 Double School Desks, @ $9 each; 100 Chairs for same, @ 50¢ each.—**25.** Sold Wm. Johnson, for Cash, 1 Mahogany Bedstead, $20; 1 Marble top Washstand, $17.—Received Cash of Robert Hall, on %, $200.—**26.** Sold John S. Williams, on %, 6 Parlor Chairs, Brocatelle, @ $5 each; 1 carved Rosewood Center Table, $50; 1 Piano Stool, $10.—Paid Cash, on Drayage %, $50.—**27.** Sold Peter Duff for Cash, 6 Office Chairs, @ $2 50¢ each.—Paid Clark Dunham, Cash in full of %, $——.—Received Cash of Robert Hall, in full of %, $——.—**29.** Sold William Dallas, on %, 1 Mahogany Sofa, $35; 1 Rosewood Arm Chair $45, 1 Hall Stand, $7; 1 Tete-a-tete, $30.

New Firm.

July 1. Jones and Mason have this day associated with them George F. Smith, who is to invest an equal amount with each of the former partners, and share equally in gains and losses. The value of unsold Merchandise is $5500; of Tools and Implements, $750; the other resources and liabilities can be ascertained by reference to the appropriate books. Mr. Smith invests: Cash,* ——.—Bo't of Henry P. Smith, for Cash, a quantity of Pine Lumber amounting to $3500.—Paid Workmen, Cash to date, $175.—**3.** Sold John S. Williams, on %, 2 Bedsteads, 1 @ $6, and 1 @ $10; 3 Washstands, @ $2 50¢ each; 6 Kitchen Chairs, @ $1 50¢ each; 1 Lounge, $15; 1 Secretary, $25; 1 Bureau, $18.—**5.** Sold E. A. Trotter, for Cash, 1 Black Walnut Book-case, $60.—Sold James Thurber for Cash, 6 School Desks, (single) @ $5 each;

* In order to ascertain the amount of Smith's investment, it will be necessary to carry the gains to the partners' accounts.—A statement should be made similar to that on page 74.

1 Teacher's Desk, $25; 2 Office chairs, @ $7 50¢ each.—**6.** Sold Joseph Wadsworth, on his note @ 30 ds., 1 Rosewood Tete-a-tete, $65; 2 Ottomans, @ $10 each.—Received Cash, in full of George Chrysler's note of the 2d ult., $61.—**8.** Paid Workmen, Cash to date, $218.—Sold James McGrath, for Cash, 12 Dining Chairs, @ $2 each; 1 Open Lounge, $17; 1 Bureau, $20.—**10.** Received Cash, on % of Wm. Dallas, $50.—Sold Steamer Troy, on %, 2 Black Walnut Sofas, @ $45 each; 3 Tete-a-tetes, @ $50 each; 24 Chairs, @ $7 each.—**11.** Received Cash, in full of E. A. Charlton's %, $——. —Sold W. F. Norman for Cash, 1 Black Walnut Book-case, $60; 1 Bureau, $30.—Bo't. of Robert Coon's for Cash, lot of Mahogany Lumber, amounting to $5700.—**15.** Paid Workmen, Cash to date, $212.—**16.** Sold Henry Harper for Cash, 50 School Desks, @ $9 each.—Received Cash of John S. Williams, on %, $90.—**17.** Sold Robert S. Hayward, on %, 1 Gothic Book-case, $75.—Received Cash of B. F. Butler, in full of %, $——.—**20.** Sold John S. Williams, on %, 12 Parlor Chairs, @ $5 each.—**22.** Paid Workmen, Cash to date, $175.—**25.** Paid Gas Bill in Cash, $15.—Sold Peter McGrath for Cash, 1 Sofa Bedstead, $50.—**29.** Paid Workmen, Cash to date, $219.—Paid Cash for rent, $100.

STATEMENT.

Showing the condition of the business, July 31.

Resources.						
Mdse. unsold,	(per Inventory,)		15000			
Cash on hand,			9826	05		
Notes "			226			
W. T. Brooks,	Balance of %		95			
John S. Williams,	" "		150	50		
Wm. Dallas,	" "		67			
Steamer Troy,	" "		408			
Robt. S. Hayward,	" "		75			
Tools and Implements, at valuation.			750		26597	55
Liabilities.						
Wm. Jones,	Net Capital, July 1,	$8637 35				
"	⅓ Net Gain,	228 50	8865	85		
Thos. Mason,	Net Capital, July 1,	8637 35				
"	⅓ Net Gain,	228 50	8865	85		
Geo. F. Smith,	Net Capital, July 1,	8637 35				
"	⅓ Net Gain,	228 50	8865	85	26597	55

QUESTIONS FOR REVIEW.

REMARKS, PAGE 50.

1. What is the peculiar feature of Set III? 2. How does the form of the Cash Book in this Set, differ from that in the preceding? 3. Which form is preferable? 4. Why? 5. For what purpose is the Sales Book used? 6. Is it essential that the sales should be entered on the Day Book? 7. How posted if not so entered? 8. What do the initials in the margin of the Sales Book indicate? 9. Is the Sales Book used in making up a list of Resources and Liabilities?

REMARKS, PAGE 72.

10. What is the purpose of Set IV? 11. Upon what grounds has Single Entry been condemned? 12. Is the objection valid? 13. Is Single Entry used to any extent in first-class Business Houses? 14. What is the important feature in this set? 15. How does the Sales Book differ in its use from that in Set III? 16. What is the advantage? 17. What do the initials in the margin indicate? 18. What other feature than the peculiar use of the Sales Book is prominent in this Set? 19. How must a change in the business be marked? 20. At what periods in business is it proper that the resources and liabilities should be shown? 21. In admitting a new partner with an equal investment, how can the proper amount of the investment be ascertained? 22. What objection to making the *new* partner's investment equal to the *original* investment of the *old*?

PART II.

DOUBLE ENTRY.

PART II.

DOUBLE ENTRY.

INTRODUCTION.

If the method of keeping accounts by Single Entry may be called a *system*, that by Double Entry may very properly claim the dignity of an exact *science;* [1] for, while the former is not devoid of excellence as a means of showing the *condition* of business, the latter not only affords a proof of its own correctness, but in addition to showing the condition of business, gives, also, with mathematical exactness, an indication of the *particular channels through which gains and losses accrue.* [2] The essential difference in the two systems has reference, mainly, to this latter qualification, and to the fact that in Double Entry all the results, including resources, liabilities, gains and losses, are shown in the Ledger, while in Single Entry, the partial results, at all attainable, are gathered from various auxiliary books, including the Ledger, Cash Book, Bill Book, etc.

[3] The *precise* difference may be appreciated by comparing Set III. in Part II. with the corresponding Set in Part I., the transactions being the same in both cases.

[4] The term *Double* Entry, as contradistinctive to *Single* Entry, has reference to the fact, that for every transaction, *two* or more entries are made in the Ledger. [5] The condition of these entries is such that each transaction, when properly recorded, will produce on the Ledger equal debits and credits; that is, the same value which is carried to the *debtor* side of one or more accounts must also be carried to the *creditor* side of one or more accounts, producing thus a perpetual equilibrium of debits and credits, [6] and affording a distinct test of the correctness of the work.

The theory of "equal debits and credits" is the leading feature of Double Entry; and although its application is, in all cases, most reasonable and satisfactory to the accountant, it is often adjudged by those whose general intelligence should cause them to blush for their ignorance in this regard, [7] as being complex and mysterious, and calculated more to befog the mind of the uninitiated than to subserve the ends of justice.

[8] To those who are troubled with these vagaries, it is only necessary to say that Double Entry contains *every feature* of Single Entry; and, that so far as Single Entry goes, it differs in none of its *results* from Double Entry; the latter being a continuation, or, rather, a perfection, of the purposes of the former. [9] The main distinction which we shall recognize between the two systems is, that while in Single Entry a record is kept of *resources* and *liabilities* only, in Double Entry a similar and additional record is kept of special *gains* and *losses*. [10] This grand feature of Double Entry should commend it at once to all prudent business men; for while it may properly be regarded as affording a true indication of the comparative merits of the various schemes of profit, it also, in a great measure, guards against errors and omissions which might pass undetected in Single Entry.

As in Single, so in Double Entry, the main book of Accounts is [11] the Ledger. [12] The Single Entry Ledger, however, contains only accounts with individuals, while the Double Entry Ledger shows the result of each transaction, both as regards the character of the exchange and the gain or loss thereby effected. Thus [13] an account is kept, not only with *persons* whom we may owe, or who may owe us, but with every *species of property* in which we deal, and every *cause* producing gain or loss.

[14] Although it is customary, in connection with Double, as well as Single Entry books, to keep a Cash Book and Bill Book, yet all the essential facts connected with cash and notes are shown in the proper Ledger accounts.

[15] The three main books used in Double Entry are the Day Book, Journal, and Ledger. [16] The Day Book and Journal are sometimes combined in one.

[17] The Day Book.

Is the original book of entry, and contains a consecutive history of the transactions, in the order and date of their occurrence. [18] It should be plain, concise, and unequivocal in its statements; neither confusing the mind by redundancy of language, nor leaving room for improper inferences from lack of sufficient explanation.

[19] THE JOURNAL,

When used separately, is the intermediate book between the Day Book and the Ledger. [20] Its office is to decide upon the proper debits and credits involved in each transaction, preparatory to their entry upon the Ledger. The process of thus classifying the transactions is called [21] *journalizing.*

[22] THE LEDGER,

Is the book of *results*,—the final book of entry. [23] Here, under appropriate heads, called accounts, are arranged all the facts necessary for a full and satisfactory statement of the business; including, not only an exhibition of the present resources and liabilities, but a distinct record of particular gains and losses. The process of transferring to the Ledger is called [24] *posting.*

The following examples of these separate books, showing their characteristic records of the same transaction, will clearly indicate their use:—

1.—Day Book.

NEW YORK, JANUARY 1, 1861.

Check mark.	Date.	Dollars.	Cents.
✓	Bought of JAMES MONROE, on account, 500 bbls. Flour..................... @ $10	5000	
	2		
✓	Sold ANDREW JACKSON, for cash, 100 bbls. Flour..................... @ $10 50	1050	

2.—Journal.

NEW YORK, JANUARY 1, 1861. Dr. Cr.

Ledger Page.	Date. (Ledger Titles.—Dr. / Ledger Titles.—Cr.)	Dr. Dollars.	Dr. Cents.	Cr. Dollars.	Cr. Cents.
1	Merchandise, Dr......................	$5000			
2	To James Monroe....			$5000	
	2				
3	Cash, Dr.....................	1050			
1	To Merchandise......			1050	

3.—Ledger.

1

DR. MERCHANDISE. CR.

Month.	Day.	For what debited.	Journal Page.	Dollars.	Cents.	Month.	Day.	For what credited.	Journal Page.	Dollars.	Cents.
1861 Jan.	1	To James Monroe..	1	5000		1861 Jan.	1	By Cash...........	1	1050	

2

DR. JAMES MONROE. CR.

						1861 Jan.	1	By Merchandise....	1	5000	

3

DR. CASH. CR.

1861 Jan.	1	To Merchandise....	1	1050							

THE SCIENCE OF ACCOUNTS.

Although the books containing a consecutive history of the business are essential for that purpose, yet [25] the *science* of Accounts pertains exclusively to the *results* of the transactions as shown in the Ledger. Particularly is this true in Double Entry, where the Ledger contains all the results necessary for a complete rendering of the condition of the business, at any time.

[26] Each Ledger Account is, properly, a statement of some financial fact, and shows one of the four following results, viz.: a *resource*, a *liability*, a *gain*, or a *loss*. These facts or results are ascertained [27] by taking the difference between the sides of the accounts, thus:

Dr. **Cash.** **Cr.**

Cash Received.				*Cash Paid out.*			
1861 Jan.	1	To Stock (Investm't)	5000	1861 Jan.	1	By Merchandise....	2500
"	15	" Merchandise.....	1500	"	10	" "	1200
"	30	" "	5000	"	30	" David Brown...	500
		$11500		"	"	" Expense........	300
						$4500	

Total Cash Received, ... $11500
" " Paid out, ... 4500
Balance on hand—[28] Resource, ... $7000

Dr. **Merchandise.** **Cr.**

Cost of Merchandise.				*Proceeds of Merchandise.*			
1861 Jan.	1	To Cash............	2500	1861 Jan.	15	By Cash............	1500
"	10	" "	1200	"	30	" "	5000
"	14	" David Brown...	1500			$6500	
		$5200					

Total Proceeds of Merchandise, ... $6500
" Cost " " 5200
Net Proceeds—[29] Gain, ... $1300

Dr. **David Brown.** **Cr.**

His indebtedness to us. *Our indebtedness to him.*

1861 Jan.	30	To Cash............		500	1861 Jan.	14	By Merchandise....		1500	

We owe him, ... $1500
He owes us, ... 500
Balance due him—[30] Liability, ... $1000

Dr. **Expense.** **Cr.**

Outlay.

1861 Jan.	30	To Cash............		300						

Total Outlay for Expenses—[31] Loss, ... $300

We will suppose the accounts given to comprise all in the Ledger, with the exception of the Stock, or Proprietor's account, which should represent the net investment; and that the net investment, as shown by the first entry in Cash account, is $5000. The following simple statement will sufficiently enforce the leading principles of the science.

Resource—Cash on hand....................		$7000	
Liability—We owe David Brown............		1000	
Net Resources, or Present Worth.....			$6000
Gain —On Merchandise............	$1300		
Loss —On Expense..............	300		
Net Gain..................		$1000	
Add original Investment.....		5000	
Gives *Present Worth*........			$6000

From the foregoing illustrations we are enabled to deduce the following general facts:

1. An Account is a [32] statement of facts pertaining to some per-

son, species of property or cause, so arranged as to show an important and specific result.

2. [33] Every account has two sides, a *debtor* and a *creditor;* each containing the results of separate transactions, and showing, in the difference between the amounts, a *general* result or fact having an important bearing upon the business.

3. [34] Accounts may be divided into two classes; one of which is used to designate the *resources* and *liabilities*, and the other, the *gains* and *losses.*

4. [35] The net gain or loss in business, as evinced by the general result of all the accounts showing gains or losses, is confirmed by a corresponding increase or diminution of wealth, which is shown in the general result of all the accounts showing resources or liabilities.

DEBITS AND CREDITS.

[36] One of the great difficulties which beset the teacher of Accounts, lies in the proper definition and enforcement of the terms "Debit and Credit." So thoroughly is this fact appreciated, that ambitious authors have been induced to prepare entire treatises on the science, claiming, as an apology for their appearance, the discovery of some "infallible rule" for journalizing, which, in the author's opinion, would entirely revolutionize the labor and processes of instruction, and open up to all future generations the grand highway of "Book-keeping-made-easy." The anxious student is assured that the whole matter turns upon the simple facts of *owing* and *being* owed. "Thus," says the author, "every *debit* owes you, and you owe every *credit;*" and from these premises is deduced the infallible and homogeneous corollary, "*Debit* what owes you, and *Credit* what you owe."

Another class of authors rush to the opposite extreme, basing the whole theory of debits and credits upon their utter *lack* of theory, announcing, at the very threshold, that "the items of which debits and credits are composed form a list of incongruous facts having no object in common." [37] And yet, these very authors, widely as they differ in the *methods* used to enforce the truths of science, would not differ in the least as to the truths themselves, when applied to the purposes of obtaining the grand *result* of any series or combination of transactions involving financial interests.

In whatever theory *we* may advance, therefore, we have no desire to underrate the honest convictions of any one who has made himself master of the subject, or to substitute our reasoning for his.

The question as to the *best methods* of presenting a truth is purely professional. The main object of every teacher should be the attainment of truth, by whatever method.

We believe that every student who will thoroughly familiarize himself with the *seven* principles which follow, will have no difficulty in deciding upon the proper debits and credits involved in any business record which he may be called upon to make:

PRINCIPLES.

1.—*The Proprietor.*

[35] The person or persons investing in the business should be *credited*, under some title, for all such investments, and also for his or their share of the gain; on the other hand, he or they should be *debited* for all liabilities assumed by the concern for him or them, for all sums withdrawn from the business by him or them, and for such loss as he or they are entitled to share.

2.—*Cash.*

[39] Cash account should be *debited* for all cash receipts, and *credited* for all cash disbursements.

3.—*Merchandise.*

[40] Merchandise, and all species of property, bought upon speculation, should be *debited*, under some appropriate head, for the cost of the property represented, and *credited* with its proceeds.

4.—*Bills Receivable.*

[41] Bills Receivable account should be *debited* with other people's notes, acceptances, and other written obligations when they become ours, and *credited* when they are paid, or otherwise disposed of.

5.—*Bills Payable.*

[42] Bills Payable account should be *credited* with our notes, acceptances, or written promises to pay, when they are issued, and *debited* when they are paid or redeemed.

6.—*Persons.*

[43] Personal accounts, such as the names of persons, banks, or other institutions, competent to sue or be sued, should be *debited* under their proper titles when they become indebted to us, or we get out of their debt, and *credited* when we become indebted to them, or they get out of our debt.

7.—*Expense, Etc.*

[44] All expenses, of whatever name, should be *debited* for the outlay, and all causes, of whatever kind, producing us value, should be *credited* under some name, for the amount thus produced.

The foregoing principles are all embraced in the following simple

Formula.

[45] *Debit* what *costs* the concern value; and *Credit* what *produces* the concern value.

QUESTIONS FOR REVIEW.

INTRODUCTION, PAGE 99

1. Why has Double Entry better claims to the distinction of an exact science than Single Entry? 2. In what particulars do the two systems differ? 3. How may the precise difference be seen? 4. To what has the term *Double* Entry reference? 5. What is the condition of every complete entry upon the Ledger? 6. What is the advantage of the equilibrium produced in the Ledger? 7. How is the theory of "equal debits and credits" sometimes viewed? 8. How may these objections be answered? 9. What is the main distinction recognised in this treatise? 10. Why should this feature of Double Entry commend it to business men? 11. What is the main book of accounts in Double Entry? 12. How does the Double Entry Ledger differ from the Single? 13. What beside *personal* accounts are kept in the Double Entry Ledger? 14. Do the Cash Book and Bill Book alone contain all the facts pertaining to notes and cash? 15. What are the three main books in Double Entry? 16. Which two of these are sometimes combined in one? 17. What does the Day Book contain? 18. What should be its character? 19. What relation does the Journal sustain to the other books? 20. What is its office? 21. What is the process of entering in the Journal called? 22. Describe the Ledger. 23. What does the Ledger contain? 24. What is the process of entering in the Ledger called?

THE SCIENCE OF ACCOUNTS, PAGE 103.

25. To what does the "Science of Accounts" exclusively pertain? 26. Of what is each Ledger account a statement? 27. How are these results shown? 28. When the *Debit* side of Cash account is the larger, what does the difference express? 29. When the *Credit* side of Merchandise account is the larger, what does the difference express? 30. When the *Credit* side of a personal account is the larger, what does the difference express? 31. When the *Debit* side of Expense account is the larger, what does the difference express? 32. What is an Account? 33. What are the characteristics of an Account? 34. Into how many classes may Accounts be divided, and what are they? 35. How is the net gain or loss in business, as shown by the special accounts, confirmed? 36. What is one of the chief difficulties in the way of teaching accounts? 37. Do intelligent authors and teachers differ in their *application* of the truths of Double Entry? 38. When should the proprietor of the business be *debited*, and when *credited*? 39. When should *Cash* account be *debited*, and when *credited*? 40. Merchandise? 41. Bills Receivable? 42. Bills Payable? 43. Personal Accounts. 44. Expense, etc. 45. Repeat the general *formula* for *debits* and *credits*.

ACCOUNTS CURRENT.

An Account Current in commercial usage, is the statement in proper form of a *current* or running account. It is usually made with a view to settlement and shows the balance due to or from the party to whom it is rendered. When large transactions are conducted on credit it is usual in rendering the Account Current to *average* the time of payment, so that the balance may be paid without either party losing interest. The various methods of averaging are given in most arithmetical works, and thoroughly enforced in the High-school edition of this series. We give below the most common form of an Account Current.

Mr. John R. Penn,

In Account Current with S. S. Packard.

1861.						
July	1	To 2 doz. Bryant & Stratton's (H.S.) Book-k'ping		30		
	"	" 1 " " " (Primary) "		7		
"	12	" 6 Webster's Unabridged Dictionary,	@ $6	36		
"	15	" 4 Reams Union Letter Paper	@ $3	12		
Aug.	10	" 1 doz. Gross Gillott's 604 Pens	@ 75¢	9		
	"	" 20 doz. Spencerian Copy Books	@ $1	20		
"	15	" 15 Dean's Commercial Law	@ $2	30		
"	20	" 20 Gross Spencerian Pens	@ 75¢	15		
"	"	" 12 Reams Best Wove Cap Paper	@ $4	48		
"	30	" 50 Commercial Arithmetic	@ 75¢	37	50	
"	"	" 6 Robinson's Surveying	$1 25	7	50	
"	"	" 12 Well's Science of Common Things	@ 50¢	6		
"	"	" 24 " Natural Philosophy	@ 75¢	18		
"	"	" 24 " Chemistry	@ 75¢	18		294
		Cr.				
July	10	By Cash		10		
"	15	" "		145		
Aug.	1	" "		50		205
			Balance due			89

SET I.

(INITIATORY.)

DAY BOOK, JOURNAL AND LEDGER.

WITH EXPLANATIONS FOR JOURNALIZING, STATEMENTS, ETC.

Business Prosperous.

REMARKS.

THE following set comprises the most simple transactions known in business; the main purpose being to illustrate the foregoing principles, and to initiate the student more fully into the processes of Book-keeping. The transactions are first recorded historically in the Day Book, in the order of their occurrence; from thence transferred to the Journal, and from thence to the Ledger. In journalizing a transaction, the first thing to be considered is, the person or thing affected; next, in what manner affected; and next, the proper application of the principle. For instance, the first entry is—" Bo't of Smith & Sons, on %, 1000 Bbls. Flour." The things affected are, Smith & Sons, and Flour. We have become indebted to the former, and the latter has cost us value by involving this indebtedness. We turn to the *principles*, and learn that personal accounts should be *credited* when we become indebted to the persons (Prin. 6), and merchandise, and all species of property, should be *debited* under some appropriate head for its cost (Prin. 3). The established form of Journal entries requires the *debit* expression to precede the *credit*, and hence we have the Journal entry—" Flour, Dr., To Smith & Sons." In posting this entry to the Ledger, we open separate accounts with Flour, and Smith & Sons, debiting the former and crediting the latter. It is not really necessary that any expression should be made under the Ledger title, the date and amount being sufficient to show the result, but it is usual to insert the *opposite* Journal expression, as an indication of the transaction. The check-mark (✓) in the Day Book is made immediately after the transaction is carried to the Journal, and the post-mark in the margin of the Journal (indicating the Ledger page to which the account is posted), immediately upon its being posted. The numeral in the Ledger column next preceding the amounts indicates the Journal page from which the amount is transferred. The Ledger is left in its current or *running* condition, the general results being first indicated by *pencil figures* on the smaller side of each account, and next, more completely and systematically in the Statement on page 121. The method of showing these results on the Ledger is fully shown in Set II.

It is expected that the student will omit no part of the exercises given, nor allow himself to proceed to a new set before fully understanding the former.

DAY BOOK,—SET I.

1

New York, January 1, 1861.

√	Bought of Smith & Sons, on %, 1000 Bbls. Flour, @ $6 00	6000
	2	
√	Sold Robert Bates, for Cash, 300 Bbls. Flour, @ $6 50	1950
	5	
√	Sold Peter Cooper, on %, 250 Bbls. Flour, @ $7 00	1750
	7	
√	Sold John Jones, on his Note @ 30 ds., 150 Bbls. Flour, @ $7 00	1050
	10	
√	Bought of J. R. Wheeler, on our Note @ 60 ds., 500 Bush. Wheat, @ $1 00	500
	12	
√	Sold James Turner, for Cash, 100 Bush. Wheat, @ $1 25 $125 00 100 Bbls. Flour, " 6 75 675 00	800
	14	
√	Paid Cash for Stationery and Books for use of Store,	50
	15	
√	Bought of Thomas Payne, for Cash, 300 Bbls. Flour, @ $5 00	1500
	17	
√	Sold Patrick Murphy, for Cash, 100 Bbls. Flour, @ $6 00	600
		14200

DAY BOOK,—SET I.

NEW YORK, JANUARY 18, 1861.

	Amount Forward,	14200
√	Bought of George Davis, on %, 1000 Bush. Oats, @ 75¢	750
	20	
√	Sold Raymond & Co., on their Note @ 5 ds., 500 Bush. Oats, @ 80¢ $400 00 100 " Wheat, " $1 15 115 00	515
	22	
√	Sold Abram Fuller, for Cash, 400 Bbls. Flour, @ $6 00 $2400 00 300 Bush. Wheat, " $1 10 330 00	2730
	25	
√	Bought of James Hathaway, on %, 1500 Bbls. Flour, @ $5 50	8250
	27	
√	Sold Jonas Clark, on %, 1000 Bbls. Flour, @ $6 00	6000
	28	
√	Received Cash in full for Raymond & Co's Note,	515
	29	
√	Sold John Drummond, for Cash, 500 Bbls. Flour, @ $5 75 $2875 00 500 Bush. Oats, " 90¢ 450 00	3325
	30	
√	Paid Clerk Hire, in Cash, $50 00 " Store Rent, 50 00	100
		36385

JOURNAL,—SET I.

NEW YORK, JANUARY 1, 1861. *Dr.* *Cr.*

		Dr.	Cr.
1	FLOUR, *Dr.*	6000	
1	To SMITH & SONS,		6000
	Flour *cost* $6000, and is *debited* according to *Principle* 3. We have become *indebted* to Smith & Sons, and they are *credited* according to *Principle* 6.		
	—— 2 ——		
1	CASH, *Dr.*	1950	
1	To FLOUR,		1950
	Cash is *received*, and is *debited*, according to *Prin.* 2. Flour has *produced* cash, and is *credited* with the amount produced, according to *Prin.* 3.		
	—— 5 ——		
1	PETER COOPER, *Dr.*	1750	
1	To FLOUR,		1750
	Peter Cooper has become *indebted* to us, and is *debited* according to *Prin.* 6. Flour has *produced* this indebtedness, and is *credited*, according to *Prin.* 3.		
	—— 7 ——		
2	BILLS RECEIVABLE, *Dr.*	1050	
1	To FLOUR,		1050
	Bills Receivable is *debited*, according to *Prin.* 4. Flour is *credited*, according to *Prin.* 3.		
		10750	10750

JOURNAL,—SET I.

	New York, January 10, 1861.	Dr.	Cr.
	Amounts Forward,	10750	10750
2	Wheat, *Dr.*	500	
2	To Bills Payable,		500
	Wheat, Dr., *Prin.* 3. Bills Pay'le, Cr., *Prin.* 5.		
	—— *12* ——		
1	Cash, *Dr.*	800	
2	To Wheat,		125
1	" Flour,		675
	Cash, Dr., *Prin.* 2. Wheat & Fl'r, Cr., *Prin.* 3.		
	—— *14* ——		
2	Expense, *Dr.*	50	
1	To Cash,		50
	Expense, Dr., *Prin.* 7. Cash, Cr., *Prin.* 2.		
	—— *15* ——		
1	Flour, *Dr.*	1500	
1	To Cash,		1500
	Flour, Dr., *Prin.* 3. Cash, Cr., *Prin.* 2.		
	—— *17* ——		
1	Cash, *Dr.*	600	
1	To Flour,		600
	Cash, Dr., *Prin.* 2. Flour, Cr., *Prin.* 3.		
	—— *18* ——		
3	Oats, *Dr.*	750	
3	To George Davis,		750
	Oats, Dr., *Prin.* 3. Geo. Davis, Cr., *Prin.* 6.		
		14950	14950

JOURNAL,—SET I.

	New York, January 20, 1861.	Dr.	Cr.
	Amounts Forward,	14950	14950
2	Bills Receivable, *Dr.*	515	
3	To Oats,		400
2	" Wheat,		115
	Bills Receivable, Dr., *Prin.* 4. Oats and Wheat, Cr., *Prin.* 3.		
	22		
1	Cash, *Dr.*	2730	
1	To Flour,		2400
2	" Wheat,		330
	Cash, Dr., *Prin.* 2. Flour and Wheat, Cr., *Prin.* 3.		
	25		
1	Flour, *Dr.*	8250	
3	To James Hathaway,		8250
	Flour, Dr., *Prin.* 3. J. Hathaway, Cr., *Prin.* 6.		
	27		
3	Jonas Clark, *Dr.*	6000	
1	To Flour,		6000
	Jonas Clark, Dr., *Prin.* 6. Flour, Cr., *Prin.* 3.		
	28		
1	Cash, *Dr.*	515	
2	To Bills Receivable,		515
	Cash, Dr., *Prin.* 2. Bills Receivable, Cr., *Prin.* 4.		
	29		
1	Cash, *Dr.*	3325	
1	To Flour,		2875
3	" Oats,		450
	Cash, Dr., *Prin.* 2. Flour and Oats, Cr., *Prin.* 3.		
	30		
2	Expense, *Dr.*	100	
1	To Cash,		100
	Expense, Dr., *Prin.* 7. Cash, Cr., *Prin.* 2.		
		36385	36385

LEDGER,—SET I.

1

Dr. *Cost.* Flour. *Proceeds.* *Cr.*

1861					1861				
Jan.	1	To Smith & Sons	1	6000	Jan.	2	By Cash,	1	1950
"	15	" Cash,	2	1500	"	5	" P. Cooper,	1	1750
"	25	" J. Hathaway	3	8250	"	7	" Bills Rec'ble	1	1050
		15750			"	12	" Cash,	2	675
					"	17	" "	"	600
		Proceeds, . . $17300			"	22	" "	3	2400
		Cost, ... 15750			"	27	" Jonas Clark,	3	6000
		Net Proceeds, $1550			"	29	" Cash,	3	2875
							17300		

Dr. *Our % against them.* Smith & Sons. *Their % against us.* *Cr.*

					1861				
		We owe them $6000			Jan.	1	By Flour,	1	6000

Dr. *Received.* Cash. *Paid out.* *Cr.*

1861					1861				
Jan.	2	To Flour,	1	1950	Jan.	14	By Expense,	2	50
"	12	" Wheat & Fl'r	2	800	"	15	" Flour,	2	1500
"	17	" Flour,	2	600	"	3	" Expense,	3	100
"	22	" Flour & Wh't	3	2730			1650		
"	28	" Bills Rec'ble,	3	515			Received, $9920		
"	29	" Flour,	"	3325			Paid out, 1650		
		9920					*On hand,* $8270		

Dr. *Our % against him.* Peter Cooper. *His % against us.* *Cr.*

1861									
Jan.	5	To Flour & Oats,	1	1750			*He owes us* $1750		

Dr. *Others' notes received.* Bills Rec'ble. *Others' notes disposed of.* *Cr.*

1861						1861				
Jan.	1	To Flour,	1	1050		Jan.	28	By Cash,	3	515
"	20	" Oats & Wh't	3	515						
		1565						Notes received, $1565 " disp'd of, 515 " *on hand*, $1050		

Dr. *Cost.* Wheat. *Proceeds.* *Cr.*

1861						1861				
Jan.	10	To Bills Payable	2	500		Jan.	12	By Cash,	2	125
						"	20	" Bills Rec'ble	3	115
						"	22	" Cash,	3	330
		Proceeds, . . $570 Cost, ... 500 *Net Proceeds*, $70						570		

Dr. *Our notes redeemed.* Bills Payable. *Our notes issued.* *Cr.*

						1861				
		Notes outstand'g, $500				Jan.	10	By Wheat,	2	500

Dr. *Outlay for Expenses.* Expense. *Cr.*

1861										
Jan.	14	To Cash,	2	50				*Outlay for Expen.* $150		
"	30	" "	3	100						
		150								

LEDGER,—SET I.

3

Dr. *Cost.* Oats. *Proceeds.* Cr.

Date						Date				
1861 Jan.	18	To Geo. Davis,	2	750		1861 Jan.	20	By Bills Rec'ble	3	400
						"	29	" Cash,	3	450
		Proceeds, . . $850						850		
		Cost, ... 750								
		Net Proceeds, $100								

Dr. *Our % against him.* George Davis. *His % against us.* Cr.

Date						Date				
		We owe him $750				1861 Jan.	18	By Oats,	2	750

Dr. *Our % against him.* J. Hathaway. *His % against us.* Cr.

Date						Date				
		We owe him $8250				1861 Jan.	25	By Flour,	3	8250

Dr. *Our % against him.* Jonas Clark. *His % against us.* Cr.

Date						Date				
1861 Jan.	27	To Flour,	3	6000				*He owes us* $6000		

GENERAL STATEMENT.

WE are enabled now to exhibit the current condition of our business during the month, with the results thus far accomplished. The Ledger accounts present the following facts:—

Dr.		**Trial Balance,—Face of Ledger.**	*Cr.*	
15750		*Cost.........* FLOUR, ... *Proceeds......*	17300	
		Our % ag'st them. SMITH & SONS, *Their % ag'nst us.*	6000	
9920		*Received......* CASH, ... *Paid out......*	1650	
1750		*His % against us.* PETER COOPER, *Our % ag'nst him.*		
1565		*Others' notes rec'd.* BILLS REC'BLE, *Other notes disp.of*	515	
500		*Cost. ....* WHEAT, ... *Proceeds. .....*	570	
		Our notes redem'd BILLS PAY'BLE, *Our notes issued.*	500	
150		*Outlay.......* EXPENSE, ...		
750		*Cost.........* OATS, ... *Proceeds......*	850	
		Our % ag'nst him. GEORGE DAVIS, *His % against us.*	750	
		Our % ag'nst him. J. HATHAWAY, *His % against us.*	8250	
6000		*Our % ag'nst him.* JONAS CLARK, *His % against us.*		
36385		..... *Equilibrium,*	36385	

The above statement is called a "Trial Balance" for the reason most apparent; it is a *trial* to ascertain if the debits and credits on the Ledger are equal, or *balance.* It does not, as some suppose, prove the Ledger to be absolutely correct, as there are many circumstances under which the Ledger may balance, and yet be wrong. This form of Trial Balance, however, is so nearly a test, that under ordinary circumstances, it may be considered satisfactory. By observing the footings it will be seen that they exactly agree with those of the Journal, which could rarely be the case, were any of the Journal entries omitted in posting; and as the footings of the Journal columns also tally with that of the Day Book, it is almost conclusive that all the original entries have found their way into the Ledger. There will remain but two chances of error in the accounts, viz: from improper Journal entries, or from posting to the wrong accounts in the Ledger.

In order to afford this additional test, we have found it necessary to carry into the Trial Balance the *total footings* of the Ledger. If we desired only to test the *balances* of the Ledger, this would not be necessary, as will be seen from the following example:

Trial Balance,—Differences.

				Dr.	*Cr.*
1	FLOUR, ...	*Net Proceeds,* . .	Gain, . . .		1550
2	SMITH & SONS,	*We owe them,* . . .	Liability,		6000
3	CASH, ...	*Amount on hand,*	Resource,	8270	
4	PETER COOPER,	*He owes us,*	Resource,	1750	
5	BILLS REC'BLE,	*Amount on hand,*	Resource,	1050	
6	WHEAT, ...	*Net Proceeds,* . .	Gain, . .		70
7	BILLS PAYABLE,	*Our notes outst'g,*	Liability,		500
8	EXPENSE, ...	*Outlay,*	Loss, . .	150	
9	OATS, ...	*Net Proceeds,* . . .	Gain, . .		100
10	GEORGE DAVIS,	*We owe him,* . . .	Liability,		750
11	J. HATHAWAY,	*We owe him,* . . .	Liability,		8250
12	JONAS CLARK,	*He owes us.*	Resource,	6000	
		Equilibrium, ...		17220	17220

We have here a test of equal debits and credits quite as satisfactory as the other, and much more brief, upon the principle of *cancellation;* that is, permitting a debt to offset a credit of the same amount, and *vice versa.* These forms have each its peculiar advantages, and it is often found convenient to combine them in one. Examples of this latter method will be found in a more advanced portion of the book.

In the Trial Balance of "*Differences*" it will be seen that each Ledger account expresses one of the four results previously mentioned, viz: a *resource*, a *liability*, a *gain*, or a *loss*. By a careful classification of these facts we are enabled to present one of the most beautiful and satisfactory theories of Double Entry, viz: that the net gain or loss in business exactly corresponds with the increase or diminution of wealth. The following statements should be carefully studied:

Resources and Liabilities.

	Resources.			
3	CASH, ...	*Amount on hand,* . . .	$8270 00	
4	PETER COOPER,	*He owes us,*	1750 00	
5	BILLS REC'ABLE,	*Notes on hand,*	1050 00	
12	JONAS CLARK, . .	*He owes us,*	6000 00	17070
	Liabilities.			
2	SMITH & SONS, .	*We owe them,*	6000 00	
7	BILLS PAYABLE,	*Our notes outstand'g,*	500 00	
10	GEORGE DAVIS,	*We owe him,*	750 00	
11	J. HATHAWAY, .	" " "	8250 00	15500
		PRESENT WORTH, . . .		1570

Gains and Losses.

	Gains.			
1	Flour, . .	*Net Proceeds,* . .	1550 00	
6	Wheat, . .	" " . . .	70 00	
9	Oats, . . .	" " . . .	100 00	1720
	Losses.			
8	Expense,	*Outlay,*		150
		NET GAIN, . . .		1570

By comparing the numerals in these statements with those in the Trial Balance, it will be seen that *all* the Ledger accounts are used, and that the original purpose of each account is fully recognized. The statement of Gains and Losses will afford a more practical idea of the peculiar advantages of Double Entry than could be gathered from any other system of logic. The bare assertion that all *gains* are the result of an *increase*, and all *losses* of a *decrease* in wealth could not be denied; but the proof of the assertion, drawn from the Ledger itself, as indicated in the above statements, will carry conviction which must be conclusive and abiding.

Commencing business without capital, it will be easily understood that the *present worth*, or *net capital* at any time, must exactly correspond with the *net gain*.

From these illustrations we derive the following

RULES.

1. *To find the Net Gain:* SUBTRACT THE SUM OF ALL THE LOSSES FROM THE SUM OF ALL THE GAINS; or, SUBTRACT THE CAPITAL AT COMMENCING FROM THE CAPITAL AT CLOSING.

2. *To find the Present Worth:* SUBTRACT THE LIABILITIES FROM THE RESOURCES; or, ADD THE NET GAIN TO THE NET INVESTMENT.

EXAMPLES FOR PRACTICE.

EXAMPLE I.—A. commenced business with the following investment: Cash in hand, $300; Cash in bank, $4000; Mdse. on hand, $5000; Notes, $2500. His losses and gains were as follows: Gain on mdse., $1575; Do. on Shipment speculations, $5000. Loss on expense, $300; Do. on bad debts, $1200. *What was his net gain? What his capital at the close of business?*

Ans.—Net gain, $5075. Cap. at closing, $16,875.

EXAMPLE II.—B. commenced business with a cash capital of $3795 83. At the end of the year his resources and liabilities were as follows: *Resources.*—Mdse. unsold, $5725; Cash on hand,

$3875 90 ; Notes, $1500 ; Personal accounts, $8500. *Liabilities*—Bills Payable, $8000; Personal accounts, $3500. *What is he worth at the end of the year? How much did he gain?*

Ans.—Present worth, $8100 90. Gain, $4305 07.

EXAMPLE III.—C. commenced business without a capital. At the end of the year his Ledger exhibited the following balances.

	Dr.		Cr.	
Cash, ...	4500			
Mdse., ...			1575	
John Johnson, ...	1500			
Robert Blake, ...	1200			
Silas Burch, ...			1875	
Andrew Smiley, ...			4725	
Bills Receivable, ...	1900			
Bills Payable, ...			1100	
Expense, ...	175			
	9275		9275	

*What has been his gain? What is his capital at the close of the year?**

EXAMPLE IV.—The following Trial Balance shows the condition of my business at the close of a year. Required a statement showing gains and losses, resources and liabilities.

	Dr.		Cr.	
Cash, ...	10397		6792	84
Merchandise, ...	5000		5620	
Real Estate, ...	10000		12000	
Andrew Simpson, ...	4000		2500	
William Matthews, ...	8000		9750	
Expense, ...	1200			
Bills Receivable, ...	7000		5000	
Bills Payable, ...			1500	
Henry Martin, ...	500		3434	16
Abram Guilford, ...	1500		1000	
	47597		47597	00

* This and the succeeding example should be rendered in the form of the Statement on page 121.

EXERCISES FOR THE LEARNER.

FIRST SERIES.

Memoranda.

January 1. Commenced business without capital. Bo't of S. S. Packard on %, Mdse. amounting to $5750.—Sold John R. Penn, for Cash, 10 Yds. Broadcloth, @ $5; 3 do. Vest Satin, @ $8.—Paid Cash for Stationery and Postage, $10.—**2.** Sold J. H. Goldsmith, on %, 1 Vest Pattern, $7 50; Trimmings for same, $2; 50 Yds. Amoskeag Sheeting, @ 12¢.—**3.** Sold J. M. Bradstreet, on his Note @ 60 ds., 1 Case Boots, 24 Pairs, @ $3 50; 25 Yds. Flannel, @ 50¢.—Sold E. A. Charlton, for Cash, 1 Box Hosiery, $10; 75 Yds. Lowell Prints, @ 10¢.—**5.** Paid S. S. Packard, Cash on %, $50.—**7.** Sold Robert Baker, Invoice of Shirting and Fancy Cloths, for $3700; Received in payment, Cash, $3000; Balance charged on %.—**9.** Paid Store Rent in Cash, $100.—Received Cash in full of J. H. Goldsmith's %, $——.—**10.** Sold James A. Packard, on %, 20 Yds. Broadcloth, @ $3 75; 50 do Cassimeres, @ $1.—**12.** Sold C. J. Dietrich, for Cash, 12 Pairs Ladies' Congress Gaiters, @ $2; 1 Case Misses' Tipped Shoes, 24 Pairs, @ $1 25; 3 Cases Men's Double Sole Boots, 36 Pairs, @ $4.—**14.** Paid Clerk's Salary in Cash, $50.—Sold J. C. Bailey, for Cash, 1 Doz. Balmoral Skirts, 12 @ $2; 1 Piece Mous. de Laine, 75 Yds., @ 20¢; 1 do. Wamsutta Sheeting, 50 Yds. @ 10¢.—**15.** Bo't of James Dawes, on our Note @ 3 mos., Invoice of Fancy Broadcloth, amounting to $2500.—Sold Rob't C. Spencer, for Cash, 2 Pieces Broadcloth, 50 Yds., @ $3 50; 1 do. Lowell Prints, 25 Yds., @ 12¢.—**16.** Paid S. S. Packard, Cash on %, $2000.—Sold Henry Ivison, on %, 150 Yds. Wamsutta Sheeting, @ 15¢; 50 Yds. Broadcloth, @ $4.—**18.** Received Cash of James A. Packard, in full of %,——.—Sold Richmond Kingman, for Cash, 3 Doz. Elastic Hoop Skirts, 36 @ $2; 4 Doz. Balmoral do., 48 @ $2 25.—**20.** Sold Henry Blakeman, for Cash, 1 Piece Irish Linen,

50 Yds. @ 75¢; 3 do. Lowell Prints, 150 Yds., @ 10¢; 5 do. Amoskeag Sheeting, 250 Yds., @ 14¢.—**21.** Sold J. C. Bryant, on %, 2 Cases Ladies' Tipped Gaiters, 48 Pairs, @ $2; 5 do. Boys' Double-sole Boots, 60 Pairs, @ $1 50.—**22.** Paid Cash for Petty Expenses, $15 50.—**25.** Rec'd Cash on Robert Baker's %, $350.—Paid S. S. Packard, Cash on %, $500.—Sold Lorenzo Fairbanks, on %, 50 Yds. Broadcloth, @ $4; 75 do. Cassimeres, @ $1 25.—**27.** Sold James Smith, for Cash, 3 Pieces Cambric Muslin, 60 Yds., @ 25¢; 3 do. Scotch Plaid, 120 Yds. @ 11¢.—Sold J. McMillan, on his Note @ 30 ds., 40 Yds. Black Doeskin, @ $1 25; 8 Pieces Merrimack Prints, 250 Yds., @ 10¢.—**30.** Sold Peter McGrath, for Cash, our entire stock of Goods, amounting, per Inventory, to $3450.—Paid S. S. Packard, in full of %, $3200.

Trial Balance.

The following Trial Balance will indicate the condition of the Ledger containing the result of the foregoing transactions.

The student should be required to render his statement therefrom after the manner of the statement in connection with Set I.

Face of Ledger.	*Dr.*		*Cr.*	
S. S. Packard, ...	5750		5750	
Merchandise, ...	8250		8971	45
Cash, ...	7747	70	5925	50
Expense, ...	175	50		
J. H. Goldsmith, ...	15	50	15	50
Bills Receivable, ...	171	50		
Robert Baker, ...	700		350	
James A. Packard, ...	125		125	
Bills Payable, ...			2500	
Henry Ivison, ...	222	50		
J. C. Bryant, ...	186			
L. Fairbanks, ...	293	75		
	23637	45	23637	45

SET II.

(In Colors.)

DAY BOOK, JOURNAL, LEDGER AND AUXILIARIES.

LEDGER CLOSED, AND RESULTS SHOWN IN AN IMPROVED FORM OF BALANCE SHEET, WITH FULL EXPLANATIONS.

Business Prosperous.

REMARKS.

THIS Set is a continuation of Set I., although the nature of the business undergoes a change. The merchandise represented in the previous Set being all disposed of, we now invest in a more miscellaneous stock, comprising a general assortment of groceries and provisions. Instead of keeping a distinct account with each article of traffic, as in Set I., we classify all under the title of "Merchandise." This is the usual business method, and should always be adopted, except where it is essential to know the gains and losses on each particular kind of property.

Having a net capital at commencement, the first entry must pertain to the existing resources and liabilities. Stock, or the proprietor, is credited with the total investment, and debited with the liabilities assumed, according to Principle 1.

The term "Sundries" is here, for the first time, used in its technical sense. It means, simply, *sundry accounts*, and is convenient as a Journal expression, and to avoid the necessity of enumerating the items which comprise the totals carried to the Ledger accounts. This convenience will be immediately apparent by comparing the Ledger entries of this Set with those of the preceding.

The object and method of "closing the Ledger" is also fully illustrated; a point which the student should not pass lightly over. The great difficulty in learning the science of Accounts from a text-book, exists in the tendency to *copy* the forms and exercises mechanically without a proper understanding of the principles which give them force.

The business aspect presented by the forms of this Set, will at once commend them to the student, as models for his emulation. The *red ink* entries, in particular, are intended to remove all the obstacles to a full and clear understanding of the instructions given.

In short, Set II. is presented as embracing, in the highest degree, the essential qualities of Double Entry; and as such, it is commended to the student's most careful attention.

DAY BOOK,—SET II.

New York, February 1, 1861.

	Commenced Business this day with the following Resources and Liabilities, taken from Ledger A. (*See Statement*, *Page* 121.)			
	Resources.			
	Cash on hand,	$8270 00		
✓	Notes " "	1050 00		
	Peter Cooper's account,	1750 00		
	Jonas Clark's "	6000 00	17070	
	Liabilities.			
	Notes outstanding,	$500 00		
✓	Smith & Sons' account,	6000 00		
	George Davis, "	750 00		
	James Hathaway's "	8250 00	15500	
	"			
	Bo't of Comstock & Co., for Cash,			
	10 Hhds. N. O. Mol., 600 gal., @ 40¢	$240 00		
	10 " Cuba Sug., 9500 lbs. " 5¢	475 00		
✓	17 Bags Rio Coffee, 1575 " " 16¢	252 00		
	20 Hf. Ch. Ool. Tea, 1080 " " 50¢	540 00		
	10 Tierces Rice, 5000 " " 4½¢	225 00	1732	
	2			
	Sold S. S. Randall, on %,			
	3 Gals. Molasses, @ 50¢	$1 50		
✓	200 lbs. Sugar, " 6¢	12 00		
	150 " Coffee, " 16¢	24 00	37	50
	3			
	Sold James W. Lusk, on his Note @ 30 ds.,			
✓	2 Hhds. Sugar, 2100 lbs., @ 6¢	$126 00		
	10 Hf. Chests Tea, 540 lbs., " 55¢	297 00	423	
	"			
✓	Paid Cash to Geo. Davis, in full of %,		750	
			35512	50

DAY BOOK,—SET II.

NEW YORK, FEBRUARY 4, 1861.

	Particulars	Rate	Items	$	¢
			Amount Forward,	35512	50
√	Sold Henry C. Spencer, on %,				
	2 Hhds. Molasses, 120 Gals,	@ 45¢		54	
	5				
√	Bo't of J. A. Tilford, on our note @ 60 ds.,				
	10 Tubs Lard, 400 lbs,	@ 13¢	52 00		
	20 Boxes Soap, 1400 lbs.,	" 7¢	98 00		
	5 Bbls. Pork, 1000 lbs.,	" 10¢	100 00	250	
	"				
√	Sold Harmer Smith, for Cash,				
	2 Bbls. Pork, 400 lbs.,	@ 10½¢	42 00		
	1 Tierce Rice, 500 lbs.,	" 5¢	25 00	67	
	6				
√	Sold B. F. Carpenter, on %,				
	2 Tierces Rice, 1000 lbs.,	@ 5½¢	55 00		
	1 Bag Rio Coffee, 150 lbs.,	" 18¢	27 00	82	
	"				
√	Bo't of Clarence Doubleday, for Cash,				
	10 Bbls. Potatoes,	@ $3 00	30 00		
	1000 lbs. Eng. Dairy Cheese,	" 18¢	180 00	210	
	7				
√	Sold James Reed, for Cash,				
	10 lbs. Coffee,	@ 18¢	1 80		
	3 Boxes Soap, 210 lbs.,	" 8¢	16 80	18	60
	8				
√	Bo't of Robert Hanaford, for Cash,				
	10 Hhds. Hav. Sugar, 11000 lbs.	@ 5¢	550 00		
	3 " N. O. " 3700 "	" 5½¢	203 50	753	50
	9				
√	Sold Henry Van Dyck, on %,				
	2 Hhds. Havana Sugar, 1970 lbs.,	@ 6¢		118	20
				37065	80

DAY BOOK,—SET II.

New York, February 10, 1861.

	Amount Forward,		37065	80
√	Paid James Hathaway, Cash on %,		4000	
	12			
√	Sold James Hathaway, on %,			
	1 Bbl. Pork, 200 lbs., @ 11¢	22 00		
	1 Bag Rio Coffee, 110 lbs, " 18¢	19 80		
	1 Hhd. Hav. Sugar, 900 lbs. " 6¢	54 00	95	80
	13			
√	Sold L. Fairbanks, on %,			
	100 lbs. Eng. Dairy Cheese, @ 25¢	25 00		
	1 Bbl. Potatoes,	4 00	29	
	14			
√	Sold Henry Van Dyck, on %,			
	10 lbs. Coffee, @ 18¢	1 80		
	50 " Eng. Dairy Cheese, " 25¢	12 50		
	50 " Rice, " 5½¢	2 75	17	05
	15			
√	Paid Cash for Rent of Store,		100	
	"			
√	Sold J. T. Calkins, for Cash,			
	150 lbs. Eng. Dairy Cheese, @ 25¢		37	50
	17			
√	Rec'd Cash of Henry C. Spencer, in full of %,		54	
	18			
√	Sold S. S. Randall, on %,			
	25 lbs. Tea, @ 56¢	14 00		
	50 " Lard, " 15¢	7 50		
	20 " Rice, " 5¢	1 00	22	50
	20			
√	Sold Peter Cooper, on %,			
	2 Bbls. Pork, 400 lbs., @ 11¢		44	
			41465	65

DAY BOOK,—SET II.

New York, February 22, 1861.

		Amount Forward,	41465	65
	Sold E. F. Hill, on %,			
√	1 Hf. Chest Tea, 54 lbs., @ 60¢		32	40
	23			
	Received of Jonas Clark, in full of %,			
√	Cash,	$3000 00		
	Note, @ 90 ds.,	3000 00	6000	
	25			
√	Paid Smith & Sons, Cash on %,		3000	
	"			
	Sold George Davis, on %,			
√	2 Hhds. N. O. Molasses, 120 Gals. @ 44⅔¢		53	60
	26			
√	Paid Cash for our Note, favor of J. R. Wheeler,		500	
	"			
	Sold E. C. Bradford, for Cash,			
√	10 lbs. Rio Coffee, @ 19¢	$1 90		
	10 " Tea, " 50¢	5 00		
	50 " Rice, " 7¢	3 50	10	40
	27			
	Sold Edwin Morgan, for Cash,			
√	1 Tierce Rice, 500 lbs., @ 6¢	30 00		
	2 Bbls. Potatoes, " 3 00	6 00	36	
	28			
√	Paid Clerk's Salary, in Cash,		100	
			51198	05

JOURNAL,—SET II.

NEW YORK, FEBRUARY 1, 1861.

1	Sundries, *Dr.*	To Stock,			17070	
2	Cash,		8270			
1	Bills Receivable,		1050			
1	Peter Cooper,		1750			
1	Jonas Clark,		6000			
	——	// ——				
1	Stock, *Dr.*	To Sundries,	15500			
3		" Bills Payable,			500	
3		" Smith & Sons,			6000	
3		" George Davis,			750	
3		" J. Hathaway,			8250	
	——	// ——				
2	Merchandise,	*Dr.*	1732			
2		To Cash,			1732	
	——	*2* ——				
4	S. S. Randall,	*Dr.*	37	50		
2		To Merchandise,			37	50
	——	*3* ——				
1	Bills Receivable,	*Dr.*	423			
2		To Merchandise,			423	
	——	// ——				
3	George Davis,	*Dr.*	750			
2		To Cash,			750	
	——	*4* ——				
4	Henry C. Spencer,	*Dr.*	54			
2		To Merchandise,			54	
	——	*5* ——				
2	Merchandise,	*Dr.*	250			
3		To Bills Payable,			250	
	——	// ——				
2	Cash,	*Dr.*	67			
2		To Merchandise,			67	
			35883	50	35883	50

JOURNAL,—SET II.

New York, February 6, 1861.

L.F.		Dr. $	¢	Cr. $	¢
	Amounts Forward,	35883	50	35883	50
5	B. F. Carpenter, *Dr.*	82			
2	To Merchandise,			82	
	″				
2	Merchandise, *Dr.*	210			
2	To Cash,			210	
	7				
2	Cash, *Dr.*	18	60		
2	To Merchandise,			18	60
	8				
2	Merchandise, *Dr.*	753	50		
2	To Cash,			753	50
	9				
4	Henry Van Dyck, *Dr.*	118	20		
2	To Merchandise,			118	20
	10				
3	James Hathaway, *Dr.*	4000			
2	To Cash,			4000	
	12				
3	James Hathaway, *Dr.*	95	80		
2	To Merchandise,			95	80
	13				
4	L. Fairbanks, *Dr.*	29			
2	To Merchandise,			29	
	14				
4	Henry Van Dyck, *Dr.*	17	05		
2	To Mdse.			17	05
	15				
4	Expense, *Dr.*	100			
2	To Cash,			100	
	″				
2	Cash, *Dr.*	37	50		
2	To Merchandise,			37	50
		41345	15	41345	15

JOURNAL,—SET II.

NEW YORK, FEBRUARY 17, 1861.

	Amounts Forward,	41345	15	41345	15
2	Cash, *Dr.*	54			
4	To H. C. Spencer,			54	
	18				
4	S. S. Randall, *Dr.*	22	50		
2	To Merchandise,			22	50
	20				
1	Peter Cooper, *Dr.*	44			
2	To Merchandise,			44	
	22				
5	E. F. Hill, *Dr.*	32	40		
2	To Merchandise,			32	40
	23				
1	Sundries, *Dr.* To Jonas Clark,			6000	
2	Cash,	3000			
1	Bills Receivable,	3000			
	25				
3	Smith & Sons, *Dr.*	3000			
2	To Cash,			3000	
	"				
3	George Davis, *Dr.*	53	60		
2	To Merchandise,			53	60
	26				
3	Bills Payable, *Dr.*	500			
2	To Cash,			500	
	"				
2	Cash, *Dr.*	10	40		
2	To Merchandise,			10	40
	27				
2	Cash, *Dr.*	36			
2	To Merchandise,			36	
	28				
4	Expense, *Dr.*	100			
2	To Cash,			100	
		51198	05	51198	05

LEDGER,—SET II.

1

Dr. Stock. *Cr.*

Date	Day	Particulars	Fol.	$	cts.	Date	Day	Particulars	Fol.	$	cts.
1861 Feb.	1	To Sundries,	1	15500		1861 Feb.	1	By Sundries,	1	17070	
"	28	" *Balance,*		2103	05			" Loss & Gain	L5	533	05
				17603	05					17603	05

Dr. Bills Receivable. *Cr.*

Date	Day	Particulars	Fol.	$	cts.	Date	Day	Particulars	Fol.	$	cts.
1861 Feb.	1	To Stock,	1	1050		1861 *Feb.*	28	*By Balance,*		4473	
"	3	" Mdse.,	1	423							
"	23	" Jon. Clark,	3	3000							
				4473						4473	

Dr. Peter Cooper. *Cr.*

Date	Day	Particulars	Fol.	$	cts.	Date	Day	Particulars	Fol.	$	cts.
1861 Feb.	1	To Stock,	1	1750		1861 *Feb.*	28	*By Balance,*		1794	
"	20	" Mdse.,	3	44							
				1794						1794	

Dr. Jonas Clark. *Cr.*

Date	Day	Particulars	Fol.	$	cts.	Date	Day	Particulars	Fol.	$	cts.
1861 Feb.	1	To Stock,	1	6000		1861 Feb.	23	By Sundries,	3	6000	

LEDGER,—SET II.

2

Dr. Cash. *Cr.*

Date			Fo.	$	cts.	Date			Fo.	$	cts.
1861						1861					
Feb.	1	To Stock,	1	8270		Feb.	1	By Mdse.,	1	1732	
"	5	" Mdse.,	"	67		"	3	" Geo. Davis,	"	750	
"	7	" "	2	18	60	"	6	" Mdse.,	2	210	
"	15	" "	"	37	50	"	8	" "	"	753	50
"	17	" H. Spencer,	3	54		"	10	" J.Hath'way	"	4000	
"	23	" JonasClark,	"	3000		"	15	" Expense,	"	100	
"	26	" Mdse.,	"	10	40	"	25	" Smith&Sons	3	3000	
"	27	" "		36		"	26	" Bills Pay'be	"	500	
						"	28	" Expense,	"	100	
						"	"	" *Balance,*		848	
				11493	50					11493	50

Dr. Merchandise. *Cr.*

Date			Fo.	$	cts.	Date			Fo.	$	cts.
1861						1861					
Feb.	1	To Cash,	1	1732		Feb.	2	By S. S. Randall	1	37	50
"	5	" Bills Payable	"	250		"	3	" Bills Rec'ble,	"	423	
"	6	" Cash,	2	210		"	4	" H. C.Spencer	"	54	
"	8	" "	"	753	50	"	5	" Cash,	"	67	
"	28	" *Loss & Gain,*		733	05	"	6	" B.F.Carp'nt'r	2	82	
						"	7	" Cash,	"	18	60
						"	9	" H.Van Dyck	"	118	20
						"	12	" J.Hathaway,	"	95	80
						"	13	" L. Fairbanks,	"	29	
						"	14	" H.Van Dyck,	"	17	05
						"	15	" Cash,	"	37	50
						"	18	" S. S. Randall,	3	22	50
						"	20	" Peter Cooper	"	44	
						"	22	" E. F. Hill,	"	32	40
						"	25	" Geo. Davis,	"	53	60
						"	26	" Cash,	"	10	40
						"	27	" "	"	36	
						"	28	" *Balan., (Inv.)*	"	2500	
				3678	55					3678	55

LEDGER,—SET II.

Dr. Bills Payable. *Cr.*

1861						1861					
Feb.	26	To Cash,	3	500		Feb.	1	By Stock,	1	500	
"	28	" *Balance,*		250		"	5	" Mdse.,	1	250	
				750						750	

Dr. Smith & Sons. *Cr.*

1861						1861					
Feb.	25	To Cash,	3	3000		Feb.	1	By Stock,	1	6000	
"	28	" *Balance,*		3000							
				6000						6000	

Dr. George Davis. *Cr.*

1861						1861					
Feb.	3	To Cash,	1	750		Feb.	1	By Stock,	1	750	
Feb.	25	To Mdse.,	3	53	60	Feb.	28	*By Balance,*		53	60

Dr. James Hathaway. *Cr.*

1861						1861					
Feb.	10	To Cash,	2	4000		Feb.	1	By Stock,	1	8250	
"	12	" Mdse.,	1	95	80						
"	28	" *Balance,*		4154	20						
				8250	00					8250	

LEDGER,—SET II.

4

Dr. S. S. Randall. *Cr.*

1861 Feb.	2	To Mdse.,	1	37	50	1861 *Feb.*	28	*By Balance,*		60	
"	18	" "	3	22	50						
				60						60	

Dr. Henry C. Spencer. *Cr.*

1861 Feb.	4	To Mdse.,	1	54		1861 Feb.	17	By Cash,	3	54	

Dr. Henry Van Dyck. *Cr.*

1861 Feb.	9	To Mdse.,	2	118	20	1861 *Feb.*	28	*By Balance,*		185	25
"	14	" "	"	17	05						
				135	25					135	25

Dr. L. Fairbanks. *Cr.*

1861 Feb.	13	To Mdse.,	2	29		1861 *Feb.*	13	*By Balance,*		29	

Dr. Expense. *Cr.*

1861 Feb.	15	To Cash,	2	100		1861 *Feb.*	28	*By Loss & Gain*		200	
"	28	" "	3	100							
				200						200	

5

Dr. E. F. Hill. *Cr.*

1861						1861					
Feb.	22	To Mdse.,	3	32	40	*Feb.*	22	*By Balance,*		32	40

Dr. B. F. Carpenter. *Cr.*

1861						1861					
Feb.	6	To Mdse.,	2	82		*Feb.*	28	*By Balance,*		82	

Dr. Loss and Gain. *Cr.*

1861						1861					
Feb.	28	To Expense,	L4	200		Feb.	28	By Mdse.,	L2	733	05
		" *Stock,*		533	05						
				733	05					733	05

Dr. Resources. Balance. Liabilities. *Cr.*

1861						1861					
Feb.	28	To Mdse.,	L2	2500		Feb.	28	By Bills Pay'ble	L1	250	
"	"	" Bills Rec'ble,	L1	4473		"	"	" Smith & Sons	L3	3000	
"	"	" P. Cooper,	L1	1794		"	"	" J. Hathaway	L3	4154	20
"	"	" Cash,	L2	348		"	"	" Stock,	L1	2103	05
"	"	" Geo. Davis,	L3	53	60						
"	"	" S. S. Randall,	L4	60							
"	"	" H. Van Dyck,	L4	135	25						
"	"	" L. Fairbanks,	L4	29							
"	"	" E. F. Hill,	L5	32	40						
"	"	" B. F. Carpen'r	L5	82							
				9507	25					9507	25

S. S. PACKARD'S BALANCE SHEET.*

Taken February 28, 1861.	*L. Fol.*	Trial Balance.		Inventory.	Representative.		Stock.		Real.	
		Dr.	*Cr.*		*Losses.*	*Gains.*	*Dr.*	*Cr.*	*Resources.*	*Liabilities.*
Stock,	1	15500	17070					1570		
Bills Receivable,	1	4473							4473	
Peter Cooper,	1	1794							1794	
Cash,	2	11493 50	11145 50						348	
Merchandise,	2	2945 50	1178 55	2500		733 05			2500	
Bills Payable,	3	500	750							250
Smith & Sons,	3	3000	6000							3000
George Davis,	3	803 60	750						53 60	
James Hathaway,	3	4095 80	8250							4154 20
S. S. Randall,	4	60							60	
Henry Van Dyck,	4	135 25							135 25	
L. Fairbanks,	4	29							29	
Expense,	4	200			200					
E. F. Hill,	5	32 40							32 40	
B. F. Carpenter,	5	82							82	
		45144 05	45144 05							
To Stock—Net Gain,					533 05			533 05		
					733 05	733 05				
To Balance—Net Capital,							2103 05			2103 05
							2103 05	2103 05	9507 25	9507 25

For full instructions in preparing this Balance Sheet, see page 147.

ORDER AND PURPOSE OF CLOSING THE LEDGER.

In the preceding Set it was thought best to leave the Ledger in its open or current condition, the *results* of the business being shown in a separate statement. When the object is to know simply the condition of the business, this method is sufficient; but when it becomes necessary to mark the progress of the business in some enduring manner upon the Ledger, the accounts must be "closed," and the *balances* exhibited, either under the account itself, or in some other account, of similar import. From the statement in connection with the previous set, the student has learned that the Double Entry Ledger contains *two* classes of accounts; one showing the *present condition* of the business, by representing all its *resources* and *liabilities*, and the other showing its *progress*, by representing its particular *gains* and *losses*. For the purpose of distinction, and as a proper designation of their character, we shall call the former of these two classes, Real, and the latter Representative. By Real accounts, therefore, is meant those which show, in the difference between their sides, either a *resource* or a *liability;* and by Representative, those which show in the same manner, either a *gain* or a *loss*. The student, if he has carefully examined the foregoing instructions, will have no difficulty in making this classification.

The object of "closing" the Ledger is to put an end to its current condition by disposing of the Representative accounts; for inasmuch as the proprietor is to be credited with his net investment, whenever that net investment is increased by gains, his account should get the benefit of it. As it would be impracticable to carry the separate gains and losses to the proprietor's account when they accrue, they are permitted to remain in the accounts producing them, until such periods as may be deemed best to transfer them. This is usually done once a year, and in some establishments every six months, thus making an era in the business, and restoring the Ledger to its proper condition of showing only resources and liabilities. We shall now attempt to take the student carefully through the process of "closing the Ledger."

PROCESS OF CLOSING.

It is supposed that the student has gone through with the process of journalizing and posting the transactions in Set II., and that his Ledger accounts present an equilibrium of debits and credits. To test this fact, before proceeding farther, we will take a

Dr. **Trial Balance.** ***Cr.***

Differences.		*Face of Ledger.*			*Face of Ledger.*		*Differences.*	
		15500		. . . Stock, ...	17070		1570	
4473		4473		. . . Bills Receivable, . . .				
1794		1794		. . . Peter Cooper, ...				
		6000		. . . Jonas Clark, ...	6000			
348		11493	50	. . . Cash, ...	11145	50		
1766	95	2945	50	. . . Merchandise, ...	1178	55		
		500		. . . Bills Payable, ...	750		250	
		3000		. . . Smith & Sons, ...	6000		3000	
53	60	803	60	. . . George Davis, ...	750			
		4095	80	. . . James Hathaway, . .	8250		4154	20
60		60		. . . S. S. Randall, ...				
		54		. . . Henry C. Spencer, . .	54			
135	25	135	25	. . . Henry Van Dyck, . .				
29		29		. . . L. Fairbanks, ...				
200		200		. . . Expense, ...				
32	40	32	40	. . . E. F. Hill, ...				
82		82		. . . B. F. Carpenter, . . .				
8974	20	51198	05	. . . *Equilibrium*, ...	51198	05	8974	20

The above form of the Trial Balance is the most comprehensive in use, and one which we would recommend for its utility. It will be seen that the footings of the "Face of Ledger" columns exactly agree with the footings of the Day Book and Journal; which affords conclusive evidence that all the transactions have found their way to the Ledger. The columns of "Differences," which must also balance, will afford a convenient test of the results of each account.

Having satisfied ourselves that the transactions have been properly posted, we now proceed to close the Ledger accounts. It must not be forgotten that the object of closing the Ledger is to present, in a proper manner, both the *present condition* of our business and its *progress.* Its present condition can be shown by a list of its resources and liabilities; and its progress by a list of its gains and losses.

By a careful examination of the facts, it will be seen that *resources* are shown by an excess of the *debit* side of REAL accounts, and *liabilities* by an excess of the *credit* side of REAL accounts; and that *losses* are shown by an excess of the *debit* side of REPRESENTATIVE accounts, and *gains* by an excess of the *credit* side of REPRESENTATIVE accounts. This will suggest the propriety of opening two accounts for these general results: one to contain the resources and liabilities, and the other the gains and losses. We will now open these accounts under the titles of "Loss and Gain," and "Balance," the former to contain the results of the REPRESENTATIVE, and the latter of the REAL accounts. Before proceeding to close the accounts, we must ascertain if they are all in a condition to show the results desired. The Merchandise account, as it now stands, shows an excess of the debit side, and would therefore represent a *loss*, if the merchandise were all sold. The account itself does not show whether the property is all sold; and the only means of ascertaining the facts in the case, is to take an actual inventory, or a valuation of that which remains unsold. When this value is ascertained, the Merchandise account should be credited with it, and Balance account debited. The Merchandise account will then be competent to show the gain or loss on merchandise. We have estimated the unsold merchandise in this case to be worth $2500, which amount we enter on the credit side of Merchandise account in *red ink*,* and transfer the same immediately to Balance account. The accounts are now in a condition to close; and we will take them in their order. The first account (after Stock, which is the proprietor's own account) is Bills Receivable. This account represents a resource consisting of other people's notes on hand; the debit side showing the notes received, and the credit side those disposed of, if any. We *close* the account by entering the difference, *in red ink*, on the *credit* side, and footing up the sides, drawing double red lines underneath. The red ink entry, or *balance*, is transferred immediately to the *debit* side of

* An entry in *red ink* on the Ledger, denotes that the amount thus writen *is to be transferred*, either to some other account, or to another position under the same account. It also shows that the entry is *first* made in the Ledger, not having passed through the usual preliminary books of entry. Red ink entries are always transferred to the *opposite side* from where they are first written, for the reason that they indicate an excess of that side.

Balance account. The next account, Peter Cooper, is closed in the same way. The next, Jonas Clark, already balances, and we close it by simply ruling the double red lines. The next, Cash account, is closed in the same manner as Bills Receivable, the balance being transferred as a resource to Balance account. The Merchandise account shows a *gain*, and the balance is transferred to the *credit* side of Loss and Gain account. Bills Payable account shows a *liability*, and the balance is transferred to the *credit* side of Balance account. Smith & Son's account also shows a *liability*, and the balance is transferred to the *credit* side of Balance account. George Davis' account shows a *resource*, and the balance is transferred to the *debit* side of Balance account. James Hathaway's account shows a *liability*, and is transferred to the *credit* of Balance. S. S. Randall's, Henry Van Dyck's, and L. Fairbank's accounts, all show *resources*, and are transferred to the *debit* side of Balance. Expense account shows a *loss*, and is transferred to the *debit* side of Loss and Gain. E. F. Hill's and B. F. Carpenter's accounts both show a *resource*, and are transferred to the *debit* of Balance.

We have now the *results* of all the accounts exhibited under the heads of Loss and Gain and Balance, and if the balances have been properly transferred, these accounts, together with the (unclosed) Stock account, must be in equilibrium. To test this, we next take a Trial Balance of these three accounts, which we call the

Second Trial Balance.	*Dr.*		*Cr.*	
Stock, ...	15500		17070	
Loss and Gain, ...	200		733	05
Balance, ...	9507	25	7404	20
	25207	25	25207	25

Having satisfied ourselves, by this test, that the balances have been properly transferred, we now proceed to accomplish the grand object of closing the Ledger, by carrying the net gain from the Loss and Gain to the Stock account. The Stock account now contains the capital invested increased by the gain, which must, of course, equal the *present worth*, as shown by the Balance account. We now close Stock account into Balance, which must produce an equilibrium of the Balance account, and complete, in that account, the record of resources and liabilities.

The Balance account is used in these Sets for its convenience in collecting, under one title, all the resources and liabilities. The same effect may be produced by bringing down the balances under the REAL accounts. This latter method is adopted in business, and particularly where the record is continued in the same Ledger.

From these remarks and applications we are prepared to submit the following order of closing the Ledger, which the student will do well to observe particularly, and to follow out in practice.

ORDER OF CLOSING.

First. Open an account with "Loss and Gain" (if not already opened), and another with "Balance," the former to contain the *losses* and *gains*, and the latter the *resources* and *liabilities.*

Second. Ascertain from the inventory if any property remains unsold; and, if so, credit each account for which such property was originally debited, with the value of that unsold, making the entry in *red ink*, "By Balance," and transferring the amount directly to the debit side of Balance account, making this entry in *black ink.* "To Merchandise," or "To Real Estate," or any other account from which the amount is transferred. The Ledger accounts will each show, now, one of the four following results, viz.: a Resource, a Liability, a Gain, or a Loss.

Third. Omitting Stock (or the Partners' accounts), commence with the first account in the Ledger. First ascertain which of the above results it shows, and make the closing entry accordingly. If the difference represent a resource or a liability, enter upon the smaller side, in *red ink*, "To," or "By Balance," as the case may be, and transfer the amount in *black ink* to the opposite side of the Balance account. If the difference represent a gain or loss, enter on the smaller side in red ink "To" or "By Loss and Gain," and transfer the amount in the same manner to Loss and Gain account. Close all the accounts (except Stock or Partners'), and transfer the balances as directed. The Loss and Gain account will now show on the debit side all the losses, and on the credit side all the gains, the difference being the net loss or net gain. The Balance account will show on the debit side all the resources, and on the credit side all the liabilities, the difference being the real interest or present investment of the proprietor or proprietors.

Fourth. Take a second Trial Balance, or a Trial Balance of the remaining open accounts: Stock (or Partners'), Loss and Gain, and Balance. If the balances have been properly transferred, the debits and credits of these accounts, taken together, must be equal.

Fifth. Close Loss and Gain account into Stock, or, if it be a partnership business, into the partners' accounts, dividing the gain or loss, according to agreement. The Stock or Partners' Accounts will now show the original investment increased by the gain, or decreased by the loss; the difference being the *present* net investment. Inasmuch as the Balance account shows the same thing, they must, of course, agree.

Sixth. Close Stock (or Partners' accounts) into Balance account, which must equalize that account, it showing now, on one side, the total resources, and on the other side the total liabilities, and presenting, in the most condensed form, the exact present condition of the business.

BALANCE SHEETS.

In commercial language a "Balance Sheet" signifies the systematic arrangement of facts, for the purpose of exhibiting at a view the condition of business. The forms in use are various, according to the necessities of the occasion or the ingenuity of the accountant. Of these the example given on page 141 comprises the most complete and symmetrical of which we have a knowledge. The following explanation will be found serviceable in preparing this sheet for the entries. The method of enforcing the facts will be apparent to any diligent student.

1. Take a sheet of paper of proper size, and for a border, rule double red lines around the margin.

2. Rule the parallel head-lines, leaving proper space for double captions, as in the example.

3. Ascertain the number of Ledger accounts to be represented; which will embrace all the accounts in the Trial Balance that do not cancel.* If the business is that of a single proprietor, usually

---

* Should there be a large number of personal accounts, it will be found difficult to include them all *separately* in this form. In such case it is customary to employ the two general titles, "Accounts Receivable," and "Accounts Payable," the one embracing all amounts owing *to* us on personal %, and the other all amounts owing *by* us. This curtailment will enable the facts of any common business to be shown in this form.

called "Stock" business, rule in pencil as many lines as will contain all the accounts and *five* additional. If it be a partnership business with two or more partners, rule three additional lines for each partner; thus, for "Stock" business, *five* lines more than all the accounts; for two partners, *eight* lines more than all the accounts; for three partners, *eleven* lines more, and so on.

4. Lay off proper spaces for debit and credit money columns; first for the footings of Ledger Accounts, second for Gains and Losses, third for Stock, or if partners, for each partner—and fourth for Resources and Liabilities; also, for a *single* money column for Inventories, and for Ledger titles and their Ledger folios. The position of these columns will be seen in the example given. These spaces can best be appropriated by using a pair of dividers, and giving each of the captions its just proportions.

5. After denoting the proper space for each heading, which can best be done with pencil, commence to rule in red ink at the right hand and bring all the lines of the two captions, "Real Accounts" and "Stock," or one of the partners, down to the lower pencil line. For the other partners drop two lines. For Losses and Gains drop two lines in Stock business, and one additional for each partner.

6. Rule the foot lines as shown, and the schedule will be ready to receive the accounts.

The process of showing results is precisely similar in its order, and the results the same as in "closing the Ledger," which has already been so fully explained as to need nothing further.

There are many kinds of business statements in use, each possessing some peculiar merit, and all having the same general purpose in view, viz: that of exhibiting the real and progressive condition of the business represented. The forms hitherto used in this work, and particularly the one on page 121, are both simple and comprehensive, and would possibly be preferred by one not versed in the processes and technicalities of Book-keeping; but we know of no form that compasses so much within such limited space, as that described above. The example, on page 141, will sufficiently indicate the points of excellence, and give the student a model for his emulation. Let him remember that in no one thing does the proficiency of a practical accountant more plainly manifest itself than in the matter of neatness in arrangement and execution. The art of *ruling* tastefully, unimportant as it may seem, is one not easily acquired nor overrated.

EXAMPLES FOR PRACTICE.

The student is requested to render statements after the form on page 141, from the following materials.

Example 1. **Trial Balance.**

	Dr.		*Cr.*	
Stock,	881		5000	
Bills Receivable,	1500		1000	
John Mason,	300		175	
Cash,	5794	67	4800	
Merchandise, (Amount unsold, $1200)	3500		2759	50
Peter Smith,	4000		1500	
Robert Pendergast,			384	
Expense,	375	83		
Bills Payable,	1500		1750	
Charles Ryan,			483	
	17851	50	17851	50

Example 2. **Trial Balance.**

	Dr.		*Cr.*	
Stock,	141	78	3000	
Merchandise, (Amount unsold, $1000.)	5000		3700	
George Hopkins,	1500		953	84
Robert Westcott,	753			
Abram Woodfall,	900			
Peter Denyse,	110		500	
Robert Rantoul,	732	98	500	
James Jackson,	75			
E. E. Ellsworth,	500		983	
Cash,	9753	20	8748	90
Expense,	450			
Commission,			183	22
Bills Receivable,	1700		150	
Bills Payable,	1500		5000	
Shipment to Detroit,	4000		4598	
Edward Rice,	700		874	
Peter Renwick,	50			
Edwin C. Packard,	900		150	
Benj. F. Holmes,	75			
F. R. Perley,	500			
	29340	96	29340	96

EXERCISES FOR THE LEARNER.

SECOND SERIES.

Memoranda.

February 1. Commenced business with the following resources and liabilities, taken from the Balance Sheet of Ledger A*—RESOURCES: Cash, $1822 20; Bills Receivable, $171 50; Robert Barker's account, $350; Henry Ivison's do., $222 50; J. C. Bryant's do., $186; L. Fairbanks' do., $293 75; LIABILITIES; our note favor of James Dawes, for $2500.—Bo't of Springer and Whiteman, on %, 20 Bags Rio Coffee, 1670lbs., @ 15¢; 15 Tierces Rice, 7500lbs., @ 4¢; 15 Hhds Cuba Sugar, 14000lbs., @ 5¢.—**2.** Bo't of Alex. Cowley, for Cash, 12 Hhds N. O. Molasses, 720 gals @ 40¢; 20 Boxes Soap, 1450lbs., @ 8¢, 10 Bbls Pork, 2000lbs, @ 10¢.—**3.** Sold Lewis Lyman on %, 30lbs., Coffee, @ 18¢; 20 do. Rice, @ 5½¢; 100 do. Sugar, @ 6¢.—Received Cash of Robert Barker, in full of %, $—— —.—**4.** Paid Cash for Stationery, and incidental expenses, $20.—**5.** Sold Alonzo Mitchell, on %, 1 Bag Rio Coffee, 80lbs., @ 18¢; 20 gals. N. O. Molasses, @ 50¢; 30lbs. Rice, @ 5½¢.—Bo't of Peter Duff, for Cash, 300lbs., English Dairy Cheese, @ 20¢; 250lbs., Butter, @ 18¢.—Sold John R. Penn, on his note @ 30 ds., 5 Boxes Soap, 350lbs., @ 10¢; 6 Bags Rio Coffee, 485lbs., @ 16¢.—**6.** Bo't of S. S. Packard, on our note @ 10 ds., 40 Hf. Chests YH Tea, 2356lbs., @ 35¢.—Sold Charles Strong, for Cash, 10 Hf. Chests Tea, 580lbs., @ 38¢; 100lbs. English Dairy Cheese, @ 22¢.—**9.** Sold Samuel Davis, for Cash, 50lbs. Butter, @ 20¢; 50lbs. Coffee, @ 18¢; 30 gals. Molasses, @ 50¢.—**10.** Sold Henry Dwight, for Cash, 30 gals. Molasses, @ 50¢; 10lbs. Rice, @ 6¢; 1 Box Soap, 75lbs., @ 10¢.—**12.** Paid Clerk's salary in Cash, $15.—Bo't of James Simpson, on %, 15 Bbls Crushed Sugar, 2520lbs., @ 10¢.—**15.** Rec'd Cash on % of Henry Ivison, $100.—Sold Thomas Hunter, on %, 5 Hf. Chests Tea, 275lbs., @ 50¢; 50lbs. English Dairy Cheese, @ 23¢; 25lbs. Rice, @ 5¢.—Sold Henry Ivison, on %, 20 gals. Molasses, @ 50¢; 3 Boxes Soap, 210lbs., @ 10¢.—**16.** Rec'd Cash in full of J. C. Bryant's %, $——.—Sold W. H. Joeckel, for Cash, 2 Bbls. Crushed Sugar, 330lbs., @ 11¢.—**17.** Sold Lewis Lyman on % 50lbs. Rio Coffee, @ 20¢; 100lbs. Crushed Sugar, @ 11 ¢.—**19.** Paid Cash in full, for our note, favor of S. S. Packard, dated, Feb. 6, due this day, $824 60.—**20.** Sold Robert Burns, for Cash,

---

* See Trial Balance, page 125.

100lbs. Crushed Sugar, @ 11¢.—Received Cash of Henry Ivison, in full of %, $153 50.—**22.** Paid James Simpson Cash in full of % $252.—Sold Philip Stone, for Cash, 4 Hf. Chests Tea, 225lbs. @ 50¢.—**23.** .Sold Thomas Hunter, on %, 50lbs. English Dairy Cheese, @ 25¢; 75 do. Crushed Sugar, @ 11¢; 15 do. Coffee, @ 20¢; 2 Boxes Soap, 140lbs., @ 10¢.—**25.** Sold Alonzo Mitchell, on %, 2 Hhds. Cuba Sugar, 1850lbs @ 6¢.—Received Cash in full for J. M. Bradstreet's note of the 3d ult., due March 5, $171 50.—**27.** Paid Cash for Store rent, $100.

STATEMENT.

The Student is expected to produce the following result from the foregoing transactions :—

Trial Balance.

Stock, ...	2500		3045	95
Bills Receivable, ...	284	10	171	50
Cash, ...	3242	50	1920	60
L. Fairbanks, ...	293	75		
Alonzo Mitchell, ...	137	05		
Merchandise, (Amount unsold, $2500.)	3036	10	961	45
Bills Payable, ...	824	60	3324	60
Springer & Whiteman, ...			1250	50
Lewis Lyman, ...	33	50		
Expense, ...	135			
Thos. Hunter, ...	188			
	10674	60	10674	60

Balance Account.

	Resources.		*Liabilities.*	
Merchandise, ...	2500			
Bills Receivable, ...	112	60		
Cash, ...	1321	90		
L. Fairbanks, ...	293	75		
Alonzo Mitchell, ...	137	05		
Bills Payable, ...			2500	
Springer & Whiteman, ...			1250	50
Lewis Lyman, ...	33	50		
Thos. Hunter, ...	188			
Stock, (Present worth,)			836	30
	4586	80	4586	80

QUESTIONS FOR REVIEW.

APPROPRIATE answers to the following queries may be found on the pages indicated. The more direct reference by figures will be henceforth discontinued.

REMARKS, PAGE 128.

1. In what sense is this a continuation of Set I? 2. What different plan is adopted in the keeping of property accounts? 3. When is it customary to keep other than a general Merchandise account? 4. When the business commences with a capital, what is the first entry? 5. What account is credited with the investment? 6. What does Stock account represent? 7. What is the technical meaning of the term "Sundries?" 8. Why is it used in Journal or Ledger entries?

ORDER AND PURPOSE OF CLOSING THE LEDGER, PAGE 142.

9. In what condition was the Ledger, Set I. left? 10. Under what circumstances is this sufficient? 11. When is it necessary to "close" the Ledger accounts? 12. When an account is closed how is the *balance* or *difference* exhibited? 13. How many classes of accounts are there in Double Entry? 14. What is the distinction? 15. What are they called? 16. What is meant by REAL accounts? 17. What by REPRESENTATIVE? 18. What is the object of closing the Ledger? 19. Why are the gains and losses in business permitted to remain in the REPRESENTATIVE accounts, instead of being carried directly to the proprietor's account? 20. How often is it customary to credit the proprietor with his gains? 21. To what condition is the Ledger restored when the gains and losses are transferred to the proprietor's account? 22. What is the first thing necessary after posting all the entries to the Ledger? 23. In what sense is the Trial Balance a test of the correctness of the work? 24. What two features are presented by the Trial Balance on page 143? 25. How may the *present condition* of a business be shown? 26. How are resources shown on the Ledger? 27. How liabilities? 28. How losses? 29. How gains? 30. What two accounts may be opened to to show these results? 31. What is contained in the Loss and Gain account? 32. What in the Balance account? 33. Can you learn from the Merchandise account the value of Merchandise unsold? 34. How is it ascertained? 35. When the Merchandise account is credited with the inventory of unsold Merchandise, what will the account represent? 36. What is the process of *closing* an account? 37. In closing an account, why is the *difference* placed on the smaller side? 38. What test have we for ascertaining if the balances of the accounts are properly transferred? 39. What accounts are contained in the "Second Trial Balance?" 40. Why will the difference in the Stock account, after the gain or loss has been transferred, equal the difference in the Balance account when all the resources and liabilities have been entered? 41. Is it necessary in closing the Ledger to open a Balance account? 42. How may the same effect be produced? 43. What is the *first* step in the order of closing? 44. Second? 45. Third? 46. Fourth? 47. Fifth? 48. Sixth?

SET III.

(Corresponding with Set III, Part I.)

DAY BOOK AND JOURNAL COMBINED.

WITH FULL STATEMENTS AND EXPLANATIONS, SHOWING THE DISTINCTIONS BETWEEN SINGLE AND DOUBLE ENTRY.

Business Adverse.

REMARKS.

THE transactions comprising this set are the same as those in Set III. Part I. and are selected for the purpose of showing the exact difference between Single and Double Entry. A careful study of the two sets in their similar and dissimilar points will open to the mind of the student a clearer distinction between the two methods of accounts than could be effected by any other form of reasoning. This distinction is most apparent in the Ledger where it will be seen that the *additional* accounts required by Double Entry relate exclusively to particular speculations, and are useful, mainly, to denote special gains and losses. If our anxiety to keep this fact prominently before the mind should lead us into unnecessary repetitions, we still think this evil less than that of leaving the point obscure.

Another decided improvement in this over the preceding Set (II.), relates to the form of the original book of entry, which here combines the Day Book and Journal. There is no doubt as to the preference of this plan over that of separate books. The only objection that can be arrayed against it is the difficulty sometimes of combining the historical with the journal expression in a manner to preserve the unity of the entry without destroying the individuality of its parts. A little practice, however, will remove this difficulty, and lead the student into a concise and symmetrical form of expression, at once comprehensive and business-like.

We have not deemed it necessary to repeat the auxiliary forms of Sales Book, Cash Book, and Bill Book, for the reason that we could suggest no improvement. Auxiliary Books are used for their convenience in classifying the departments of business, and do not pertain necessarily to any particular theory or method of accounts. In Single Entry, however, they are often essential in preserving a sufficient record of resources and liabilities, which in Double Entry are shown independently in the Ledger.

The manner of *closing* the accounts differs from Set II. only in bringing down the resources and liabilities under the accounts themselves, instead of transferring them to a separate account like "Balance." A few of the accounts, containing only *one* item, are unnecessarily closed, and the balances brought down. This plan is sometimes adopted in business, for the purpose of exhibiting the condition of affairs on the Ledger *at some certain date.*

The method of showing general results through a detailed statement is commended to the careful attention of the student.

JOURNAL DAY BOOK,—SET III.

ALBANY, JULY 1, 1861.

L.F.		Dr.		Cr.
1	SUNDRIES, *Dr.* To H. B. BRYANT,			9075
	For Investment, as follows.			
1	MERCHANDISE, As per Inventory,	4750		
2	BILLS REC'BLE, " " Bill Book,	1500		
2	CASH, " " Cash Book,	1200		
2	JOHN R. PENN, Balance of %,	500		
3	L. FAIRBANKS, " "	750		
3	ALONZO GASTON, " "	375		
	//			
1	SUNDRIES, *Dr.* To H. D. STRATTON,			8000
	For Investment, as follows.			
3	REAL ESTATE, House and lot, val. at,	5000		
2	CASH,* Am't in Union Bank,	3000		
	//			
3	EXPENSE, *Dr.*	5		
2	To CASH,			5
	Paid for postage stamps, pens, &c.,			
	//			
2	CASH, *Dr.*	39		
1	To MERCHANDISE,			39
	Sold Robt. Van Schaick, per S.B.,			
	2			
1	CASH, *Dr.*	250		
2	To JOHN R. PENN,			250
	Received on %,			
	//			
3	EXPENSE, *Dr.*	10		
2	To CASH,			10
	Paid for printing Hand-Bills			
		17379		17379

* Some houses keep a regular Bank account in their main books, debiting the bank with deposits, and crediting it with checks drawn, while others keep the account only in an auxiliary book, and count the cash in bank the same as that in safe. We have in this instance adopted the latter plan.

JOURNAL DAY BOOK,—SET III.

ALBANY, JULY 3, 1861.

L.F.		Dr. $	cts.	Cr. $	cts.
	Amounts Forward,	17379		17379	
4	JAMES JOHNSON, *Dr.*	192			
1	To MERCHANDISE,			192	
	Per Sales Book,				
	//				
2	CASH, *Dr.*	17	50		
1	To MERCHANDISE,			17	50
	Petty sales, per C.B.,				
	4				
2	BILLS RECEIVABLE, *Dr.*	108	20		
1	To MERCHANDISE,			108	20
	Sold E. H. Bender, per S.B.,				
	//				
3	EXPENSE, *Dr.*	175			
2	To CASH,			175	
	Paid C. Jones, repair'g store,				
	5				
1	MERCHANDISE, *Dr.* To SUNDRIES,	1359	50		
4	To CLAFFLIN MELLEN & CO., Invoice of Boots and Shoes,			575	
4	" A. T. STEWART & CO., Invoice of Dry Goods,			757	
2	" CASH, Paid freight on above,			27	50
	7				
4	E. B. RICE, *Dr.*	42	45		
1	To MERCHANDISE,			42	45
	Per Sales Book,				
	//				
2	CASH, *Dr.*	375			
3	To ALONZO GASTON,			375	
	Received in full of %,	19648	65	19648	65

JOURNAL DAY BOOK,—SET III.

Albany, July 7, 1861.

		Dr. $	cts.	Cr. $	cts.
	Amounts Forward,	19648	65	19648	65
3	Expense, *Dr.*	25			
2	To Cash,			25	
	Paid Clerk hire,				
	8				
2	Cash, *Dr.*	19	82		
1	To Merchandise,			19	82
	Sold W. H. Clark, per S.B.,				
	"				
3	Expense, *Dr.*	15	75		
2	To Cash,			15	75
	Paid expenses to N.Y.,				
	10				
4	Benjamin Payn, *Dr.*	23	41		
1	To Merchandise,			23	41
	Per Sales Book,				
	"				
2	Cash, *Dr.*	500			
2	To Bills Receivable,			500	
	In full of Robt. Bruce's note,				
	"				
4	A. T. Stewart & Co., *Dr.*	300			
2	To Cash,			300	
	Paid them on %,				
	"				
2	Bills Receivable, *Dr.*	173			
1	To Merchandise,			173	
	Sold C. S. Sill, per S.B.,	20705	63	20705	63

JOURNAL DAY BOOK,—SET III.

Albany, July 12, 1861.

	Amounts Forward,	20705	63	20705	63
1	H. D. Stratton, *Dr.*	75			
5	To Bills Payable,			75	
	Accepted draft, favor of P. R. Spencer, per B.B.,				
	— // —				
2	Cash, *Dr.*	33	50		
1	To Merchandise,			33	50
	Received for petty sales, per C.B.,				
	— // —				
5	Amos Dean, *Dr.*	180			
1	To Merchandise,			180	
	Per Sales Book,				
	— 13 —				
4	Clafflin, Mellen & Co., *Dr.*	575			
5	To Bills Payable,			575	
	Our note to balance %,				
	— 15 —				
4	H. B. Bryant, *Dr.*	75			
2	To Cash,			75	
	Paid him on %,				
	— // —				
2	Cash, *Dr.*	350			
3	To L. Fairbanks,			350	
	Received on %,				
	— 18 —				
2	Cash, *Dr.*	252			
1	To Merchandise,			252	
	Sold G. H. Doty, per S.B.,	22246	13	22246	13

JOURNAL DAY BOOK,—SET III.

ALBANY, JULY 19, 1861.

	Amounts Forward,	22246	13	22246	13
3	EXPENSE, *Dr.*	15			
2	To CASH,			15	
	Paid for Advertisements in Evening Journal,				
	20				
5	VICTOR M. RICE, *Dr.*	82	88		
1	To MERCHANDISE,			82	88
	Per Sales Book,				
	"				
2	CASH, *Dr.*	30			
5	To VICTOR M. RICE			30	
	Received on %,				
	"				
3	EXPENSE, *Dr.*	10			
2	To CASH,			10	
	Paid petty expenses per C.B.				
	21				
2	CASH, *Dr.*	50			
5	To AMOS DEAN,			50	
	Received on %,				
	"				
3	EXPENSE, *Dr.*	183			
2	To CASH,			183	
	Bill of Carpenter work $175 Drayage, $5; Porterage, $3				
	22				
2	BILLS RECEIVABLE, *Dr.*	339			
1	To MERCHANDISE,			339	
	Sold J. R. Morgan, per S.B.				
		22956	01	22956	01

JOURNAL DAY BOOK,—SET III.

Albany, July 23, 1861.

	Amounts Forward,	22956	01	22956	01
6	James Shelden, *Dr.*	132	24		
1	To Merchandise,			132	24
	Per Sales Book,				
	— // —				
2	Cash, *Dr.*	234			
1	To Merchandise,			234	
	Sold R. Metcalf, per S.B.,				
	— *24.* —				
2	Cash, *Dr.*	106			
1	To Merchandise,			106	
	Sold Chas. Heydon, per S.B.				
	— // —				
2	Cash, *Dr.*	42	45		
4	To E. B. Rice,			42	45
	Received in full of %,				
	— *25* —				
5	William Shepard, *Dr.*	37	55		
1	To Merchandise,			37	55
	Per Sales Book,				
	— // —				
2	Cash, *Dr.*	163	20		
1	To Merchandise,			163	20
	Sold Robt. Dawes, per S.B.,				
	— // —				
5	Bills Payable, *Dr.*	75			
2	To Cash,			75	
	Paid on Accept. fav. H.D.S.				
	— // —				
3	Expense, *Dr.*	25			
2	To Cash,			25	
	Paid Clerk hire,	23771	45	23771	45

ALBANY, JULY 26, 1861.

	Amounts Forward,	23771	45	23771	45
6	JOHN BELDEN, *Dr.*	216	50		
1	To MERCHANDISE,			216	50
	Per Sales Book,				
	″				
4	A. T. STEWART & Co., *Dr.*	457			
2	To CASH,			457	
	Paid them in full of %,				
	27				
2	CASH, *Dr.*	138	72		
1	To MERCHANDISE,			138	72
	Sold J. H. Lansley, per S.B.				
	29				
2	CASH, *Dr.*	154			
1	To MERCHANDISE,			154	
	Sold W. H. Fiquet, per S.B.				
	″				
2	CASH, *Dr.*	250			
2	To JOHN R. PENN,			250	
	Received in full of %,				
	20				
1	SUNDRIES, *Dr.* To MERCHANDISE,			182	40
	Sold Chas. A. Seeley, p'r S.B				
2	CASH, Amount received,	75			
6	CHAS. A. SEELEY, Balance on %,	107	40		
		25170	07	25170	07

LEDGER,—SET III.

Dr. H. B. Bryant. *Cr.*

1861						1861					
July	15	To Cash,	4	75		July	1	By Sundries,	1	9075	
"	31	" Loss & Gain	L6	352	94						
"	"	" *Balance,*	L1	8647	06						
				9075	00					9075	
						Aug	1	By Balance,	L1	8647	06

Dr. H. D. Stratton. *Cr.*

1861						1861					
July	12	To Bills Payable	4	75		July	1	By Sundries,	1	8000	
"	31	" Loss & Gain,	L6	352	94						
"	31	" *Balance,*	L1	7572	06						
				8000	00					8000	00
						Aug	1	By Balance,	L1	7572	06

Dr. Merchandise. *Cr.*

1861						1861					
July	1	To H. B. Bryant	1	4750		July	1	By Cash,	1	39	
"	5	" Sundries,	2	1359	50	"	3	" J. Johnson,	2	192	
						"	"	" Cash,	"	17	50
						"	4	" Bills Rec'ble,	"	108	20
						"	7	" E. B. Rice,	"	42	45
						"	8	" Cash,	3	19	82
						"	10	" Benj. Payn,	"	23	41
						"	12	" Bills Rec'ble,	"	173	
						"	"	" Cash,	4	33	50
						"	13	" Amos Dean,	"	180	
						"	18	" Cash,	"	252	
						"	20	" Vict. M. Rice	5	82	88
						"	22	" Bills Rec'ble,	"	339	
						"	23	" Jas. Shelden,	6	132	24
						"	"	" Cash,	"	234	
						"	24	" "	"	106	
						"	25	" W. Shepard,	"	37	55
						"	"	" Cash,	"	163	20
						"	26	" John Belden,	7	216	50
						"	27	" Cash,	"	138	72
						"	29	" "	"	154	
						"	30	" Sundries,	"	182	40
						"	"	" *Balance,*	L1	3000	
						"	"	" *Loss & Gain,*	L6	242	13
				6109	50					6109	50
Aug	1	To Balance,	L1	3000							

Dr. Bills Receivable. Cr.

Date			Fol.	$	cts.	Date			Fol.	$	cts.
1861						1861					
July	1	To H. B. Bryant,	1	1500		July	10	By Cash,	3	500	
"	4	" Mdse.,	2	108	20		31	" *Balance,*	L 2	1620	20
"	12	" "	3	173							
"	22	" "	5	339							
				2120	20					2120	20
Aug	1	To Balance,		1620	20						

Dr. John R. Penn. Cr.

Date			Fol.	$	cts.	Date			Fol.	$	cts.
1861						1861					
July	1	To H. B. Bryant,	1	500		July	2	By Cash,	1	250	
						"	29	" "	7	250	
				500						500	

Dr. Cash. Cr.

Date			Fol.	$	cts.	Date			Fol.	$	cts.
1861						1861					
July	1	To H. B. Bryant,	1	1200		July	1	By Expense,	1	5	
"	"	" H.D.Stratton	"	3000		"	2	" "	"	10	
"	"	" Mdse.,	"	39		"	4	" "	2	175	
"	2	" J. R. Penn,	"	250		"	5	" Mdse.,	"	27	50
"	3	" Mdse.,	2	17	50	"	7	" Expense,	3	25	
"	7	" A. Gaston,	"	375		"	8	" "	"	15	75
"	8	" Mdse.,	3	19	82	"	10	" A.T.Stw.&Co	"	300	
"	10	" Bills Rec'ble,	"	500		"	15	" H. B. Bryant,	4	75	
"	12	" Mdse.,	4	33	50	"	19	" Expense,	5	15	
"	16	" L. Fairbanks,	"	350		"	20	" "	"	10	
"	18	" Mdse.,	"	252		"	21	" "	"	183	
"	20	" V. M. Rice,	5	30		"	25	" Bills Payable	6	75	
"	21	" Amos Dean,	"	50		"	"	" Expense,	"	25	
"	23	" Mdse.,	6	234		"	26	" A.T.Stw.&Co	7	457	
"	24	" "	"	106		"	31	*By Balance,*	L 2	5881	94
"	"	" E. B. Rice,	"	42	45						
"	25	" Mdse.,	"	163	20						
"	27	" "	7	138	72						
"	29	" "	"	154							
"	"	" J. R. Penn,	"	250							
"	30	" Mdse.,	"	75							
				7280	19					7280	19
Aug	1	To Balance,		5881	94						

LEDGER,—SET III.

3

Dr. L. Fairbanks. *Cr.*

Date			Fo.	$	cts.	Date			Fo.	$	cts.
1861 July	1	To H. B. Bryant,	1	750		1861 July	16	By Cash,	4	350	
						"	31	" *Balance,*	L 3	400	
				750						750	
Aug	1	To Balance,		400							

Dr. Alonzo Gaston. *Cr.*

Date			Fo.	$	cts.	Date			Fo.	$	cts.
1861 July	1	To H. B. Bryant,	1	375		1861 July	7	By Cash,	2	375	

Dr. Real Estate. *Cr.*

Date			Fo.	$	cts.	Date			Fo.	$	cts.
1861 July	1	To H. B. Bryant,	1	5000		1861 *July*	31	*By Balance,*	L 3	5000	
Aug	1	To Balance,		5000							

Dr. Expense. *Cr.*

Date			Fo.	$	cts.	Date			Fo.	$	cts.
1861 July	1	To Cash,	1	5		1861 *July*	31	*By Loss & Gain*	L 6	463	75
"	2	" "	"	10							
"	4	" "	2	175							
"	7	" "	3	25							
"	8	" "	"	15	75						
"	19	" "	5	15							
"	20	" "	"	10							
"	21	" "	"	183							
"	25	" "	6	25							
				463	75					463	75

Dr. James Johnson. *Cr.*

				$	c					$	c
1861 July	3	To Mdse.,	2	192		1861 *July*	31	*By Balance,*	L4	192	
Aug	1	To Balance,		192							

Dr. Claflin, Mellen & Co. *Cr.*

				$	c					$	c
1861 July	15	To Bills Payable	4	575		1861 July	5	By Mdse.,	2	575	

Dr. A. T. Stewart & Co. *Cr.*

				$	c					$	c
1861 July	10	To Cash,	3	300		1861 July	5	By Mdse.,	2	757	
"	26	" "	7	457							
				757						757	

Dr. E. B. Rice. *Cr.*

				$	c					$	c
1861 July	7	To Mdse.,	2	42	45	1861 July	24	By Cash,	6	42	45

Dr. Benjamin Payn. *Cr.*

				$	c					$	c
1861 July	10	To Mdse.,	3	23	41	1861 *July*	31	*By Balance,*	L4	23	41
Aug	1	To Balance,		23	41						

LEDGER,—SET III.

5

Dr. Bills Payable. *Cr.*

1861						1861					
July	25	To Cash,	6	75		July	12	By H. D. Strat'n	4	75	
"	31	" *Balance,*	L5	575		"	15	" Claf. M. & Co.	"	575	
				650						650	
						Aug	1	By Balance,	L5	575	

Dr. Amos Dean. *Cr.*

1861						1861					
July	13	To Mdse.,	4	180		July	21	By Cash,	5	50	
						"	31	" *Balance,*	L5	130	
				180						180	
Aug	1	To Balance,	L5	130							

Dr. Victor M. Rice. *Cr.*

1861						1861					
July	20	To Mdse.,	5	82	88	July	20	By Cash,	5	30	
						"	31	" *Balance,*	L5	52	88
				82	88					82	88
Aug	1	To Balance,	L5	52							

Dr. James Shelden. *Cr.*

1861						1861					
July	23	To Mdse.;	6	132	24	*July*	31	*By Balance,*	L5	132	24
Aug	1	To Balance,	L5	132	24						

Dr. William Shepard. *Cr.*

1861						1861					
July	25	To Mdse.,	6	37	55	*July*	31	*By Balance,*	L5	37	55
Aug	1	To Balance,	L5	37	55						

LEDGER—SET III.

Dr. John Belden. Cr.

1861				$	c	1861				$	c
July	26	To Mdse.,	7	216	50	*July*	31	*By Balance,*	L 6	216	50
Aug	1	To Balance,	L6	216	50						

Dr. Cha's A. Seeley. Cr.

1861				$	c	1861				$	c
July	30	To Mdse.,	7	107	40	*July*	31	*By Balance,*	L 6	107	40
Aug	1	To Balance,	L6	107	40						

Dr. Loss and Gain. Cr.

1861				$	c	1861				$	c
July	31	To Mdse.,	L1	242	13	*July*	31	*By H. B. Bryant*	L 1	352	94
"	"	" Expense,	L3	463	75	"	"	" *H. D. Strat'n*	L 1	352	94
				705	88					705	88

STATEMENT.

The following detailed statement should be carefully compared with the Single Entry Statement on page 67, that the characteristic features of the two systems may be thoroughly appreciated. We have designated the Real and Representative accounts in the Trial Balance and have included *all* the Ledger accounts, that the general footings may be made to agree with the footings of the Journal. In rendering the Statement, those accounts which cancel or balance, are, of course, omitted. With this form of Trial Balance it would scarcely be necessary to do more than carry the *balances* of the accounts into the statement columns as in the Statement on page 121; but this form gives the philosophy more in detail.

Trial Balance.

				Total Footings.				Balances.			
				Dr.		*Cr.*		*Dr.*		*Cr.*	
1	H. B. Bryant,	*Real,*		75		9075				9000	
2	H. D. Stratton,	*Real,*		75		8000				7925	
3	Merchandise,	*Rep.,*		6109	50	2867	37	3242	13		
4	Bills Receivable,	*Real,*		2120	20	500		1620	20		
5	John R. Penn,	*Real,*	(*Canceled.*)	500		500					
6	Cash,	*Real,*		7280	19	1398	25	5881	94		
7	L. Fairbanks,	*Real,*		750		350		400			
8	Alonzo Gaston,	*Real,*	(*Canceled.*)	375		375					
9	Real Estate,	*Rep.,*		5000				5000			
10	Expense,	*Rep.,*		463	75			463	75		
11	James Johnson,	*Real,*		192				192			
12	Claf., Mellen & Co,	*Real,*	(*Canceled.*)	575		575					
13	A. T. Stewart,	*Real,*	(*Canceled.*)	757		757					
14	E. B. Rice,	*Real,*	(*Canceled.*)	42	45	42	45				
15	Benjamin Payn,	*Real,*		23	41			23	41		
16	Bills Payable,	*Real,*		75		650				575	
17	Amos Dean,	*Real,*		180		50		130			
18	Victor M. Rice,	*Real,*		82	88	30		52	88		
19	James Shelden,	*Real,*		132	24			132	24		
20	William Shepard,	*Real,*		37	55			37	55		
21	John Belden,	*Real,*		216	50			216	50		
22	Chas. A. Seeley,	*Real,*		107	40			107	40		
				25170	07	25170	07	17500	00	17500	00

Inventory,

Mdse. unsold, ... $3000

Real Estate, ... 5000

STATEMENT.

Losses and Gains.—Representative Accounts.

				Losses.		Gains.	
3	MERCHANDISE,	*Cost,*	$6109 50				
		Proc.—Sales, $2867 37					
		Value unsold, 3000 00	5867 37				
		Net loss, . .		242	13		
10	EXPENSE,	*Outlay for Expenses,*		463	75		
		TOTAL NET LOSS, . .				705	88
		H. B. B's., ½ net loss, .	$352 94	705	88	705	88
		H.D.Strat., " "	352 94				

Resources and Liabilities.—Real Accounts.

				Resources.		Liabilities.	
	1. *From Inventories of unsold property.*						
	MERCHANDISE,			3000			
	REAL ESTATE,			5000			
	2. *From Ledger Accounts.*						
4	BILLS RECEIVABLE,	*Others' notes received,*	$2120 20				
		" " *dis. of,*	500 00				
		" " *on hand,*		1620	20		
6	CASH,	*Amount received,* . .	$7280 19				
		" *paid out,* . .	1398 25				
		" *on hand,* . .		5881	94		
7	L. FAIRBANKS,	*Our % against him,*	$750 00				
		His " " *us,* .	350 00				
		He owes us, ...		400			
11	JAMES JOHNSON,	*He owes us,*		192			
15	BENJ. PAYN,	" " "		23	41		
16	BILLS PAYABLE,	*Our notes issued,* . .	$650 00				
		" " *redeemed,*	75 00				
		" " *outstand'g,*				575	
17	AMOS DEAN,	*Our % against him,*	$180 00				
		His " " *us,* .	50 00				
		He owes us, ...		130			
18	VICTOR M. RICE,	*Our % against him,*	$82 88				
		His " " *us,* .	30 00				
		He owes us, ...		52	88		
19	JAMES SHELDEN,	" " "		132	24		
20	WILLIAM SHEPARD,	" " "		37	55		
21	JOHN BELDEN,	" " "		216	50		
22	CHAS. A. SEELEY,	" " "		107	40		
1	H. B. BRYANT,	*His net investment,* .	$9000 00				
		" " *loss,*	352 94				
		HIS PRESENT INTEREST.				8647	06
2	H. D. STRATTON,	*His net investment,* .	$7925 00				
		" " *loss,*	352 94				
		HIS PRESENT INTEREST,				7572	06
				16794	12	16794	12

EXAMPLES FOR PRACTICE.

THE following examples are to be rendered in the form of the Statement on page 169.

EXAMPLE 1. **Trial Balance.**

	Dr.		Cr.	
Warren P. Spencer, (Partner,) . .	700		5724	58
J. C. Bryant, . . do. . .			5024	58
Merchandise, (Amount unsold, $5000,)	12000		7594	
Cash, ...	15752	25	9692	84
Bills Receivable, ...	4000		1500	
Bills Payable, ...	9000		12000	
E. G. Folsom, ...	750			
E. R. Felton, ...	123	75	965	
Expense, ...	175			
	42501	00	42501	00

EXAMPLE 2. **Trial Balance.**

	Dr.		Cr.	
James W. Lusk, (Partner,) . . .			4500	
H. W. Ellsworth, do. . . .	398	72	5000	
H. C. Spencer, . . do. . . .			4500	
Cash, ...	17594	28	15329	50
Bills Receivable, ...	7500		4300	
Merchandise, (Inventory, $1000,) .	6794		5382	50
Real Estate, (do. 5000,) .	5000		125	
Expense, ...	150			
Bills Payable, ...	4000		5700	
Robert Paton, ...	2000			
Samuel Ogden, ...	1400			
	44837	00	44837	00

QUESTIONS FOR REVIEW.

REMARKS, PAGE 154.

1. What is the purpose of Set III? 2. With what previous set does it correspond? 3. Where is the distinction between Single and Double Entry most apparent? 4. To what do the *additional* accounts in Double Entry relate? 5. For what are they useful? 6. What improvement has this set over Set II? 7. What is the objection usually urged against combining the Day Book and Journal? 8. What is the general purpose of auxiliary books? 9. For what are they used in Single Entry? 10. In what does the method of closing the accounts in this Ledger differ from the preceding? 11. Is it usual to *bring down* single items in the Ledger? 12. When is this proper?

NOTE.—Let this set be followed by the "Exercises" on page 69.

SET IV.

GENTLEMEN'S FURNISHING BUSINESS.

(PARTNERSHIP.)

JOURNAL, CASH BOOK, AND SALES BOOK, USED AS PRINCIPAL BOOKS.

Business Prosperous.

REMARKS.

THE characteristic feature of this set consists in the peculiar arrangement and use of the original books of entry. Hitherto the transactions, whatever auxiliary books have been used, have all been entered in the Journal, and from thence posted to the Ledger. This plan, although having some advantages, is objectionable upon the ground of too much labor, nearly all the transactions being entered twice or more before being carried to the Ledger.

The plan of posting directly from the original books of entry, such as the Cash Book, Sales Book, etc., is not only practical and business-like, but serves, in the most striking manner to enforce the theory of the science, and to disarm that class of objectionists who insist that Double Entry requires vastly more writing than Single Entry.

The only difficulty in the way of posting directly from the original books lies in the danger of conflicting the entries, or posting the same amounts *twice*. For instance, the debit side of the Cash Book comprises in itself a double entry, which is equivalent to the Journal entry "Cash Dr. To Sundries." In posting from the Cash Book, the total of the *debit* side is carried to the Cash account in the Ledger, and the item comprising that amount to the *credit* side of the various accounts mentioned, among which is Merchandise. It is very evident that if all the Merchandise sold be credited from the Sales Book, the amount sold for cash would be credited *twice*, hence the necessity of an extra column in the Sales Book for Cash sales which are omitted in posting from the Sales Book. The special "Mdse." and "Expense" columns in the Cash Book are to save the necessity of so many special entries to these accounts in the Ledger. The method of posting from the Cash and Sales Books is extremely simple. The amounts in the "General" column of the Cash Book may be posted at any time—the page of the Ledger being indicated in the margin, the "Mdse." and "Expense" columns at the end of the month, or as often as it may be best to close the Cash Book. The sales for Cash are marked "C.B." in the margin of the Sales Book, and the amounts extended into the "Cash" column. The other accounts from the Sales Book may be posted at any time, the page of the Ledger being indicated in the margin. The sales for notes are marked *inside* the margin, "B.R." and, of course, posted to Bills Receivable account. Instead of indicating the page from which the transactions are posted, the initials of the original book are given in the Ledger.

JOURNAL,—SET IV.

CHICAGO, SEPTEMBER 1, 1861.

2	Merchandise,	6750			
1	To J. R. Penn,			6750	
	Am't invested, per Inventory				
	—— " ——				
1	J. R. Penn,	1750			
3	To Bills Payable,			1750	
	Assumed for him,				
	—— " ——				
1	Sundries, To J. C. Bryant,			5900	
	Amounts invested,				
1	Bills Rec'ble, J. Smith's note, $750 00				
	H. Young's, " 750 00	1500			
1	J. T. Calkins, Balance of %,	500			
2	E. R. Felton, do.	376			
2	J. H. Goldsmith, "	1170			
2	Jas. Atwater, "	1250			
3	P. C. Schuyler, "	1104			
	—— " ——				
1	J. C. Bryant, To Sundries,	900			
	Liabilities assumed,				
3	To Chas. Taylor, Bal. of %,			500	
3	J. W. Lusk, "			400	
	—— 15 ——				
3	J. W. Lusk,	400			
3	To Bills Payable,			400	
	Our note @ 30 ds. to Bal. %				
	—— 20 ——				
1	Bills Receivable,	1104			
3	To P. C. Schuyler,			1104	
	His note @ 60 ds. to Bal. %	16804	00	16804	00

CASH BOOK,—

1861 Cash. *Dr.*

Sept.				*Mdse.*		*General.*	
1	1	S. S. Packard, . .	Am't invested, ...			5000	
	✓	Mdse., ...	T. W. W. Sales Book, .	363	72		
	✓	Mdse., ...	Petty Sales. P. C. B., .	54	25		
2	1	J. T. Calkins, . .	On %, ...			200	
3	✓	Mdse., ...	D. V. B. Sales Book, . .	89			
"	✓	Mdse., ...	Petty Sales. P. C. B., .	28	90		
5	✓	Mdse., ...	" " " . .	105			
7	✓	Mdse., ...	J. A. Sales Book, . . .	737	50		
10	2	James Atwater, .	On %, ...			750	
12	✓	Mdse., ...	Petty Sales. P. C. B., .	58			
14	✓	Mdse., ...	" " " . .	138			
15	✓	Mdse., ...	W. B. Sales Book, . .	128	25		
16	1	J. T. Calkins, . .	On %, ...			150	
17	1	Bills Receivable, .	J. Smith's note, ...			750	
"	3	Interest, ...	On same, ...			34	25
18	✓	Mdse., ...	Petty Sales. P. C. B., .	94	83		
22	2	J. H. Goldsmith, .	On %, ...			1000	
"	✓	Mdse., ...	Petty Sales. P. C. B., .	112	44		
25	2	E. R. Felton, . .	In full, ...			376	
"	✓	Mdse., ...	Petty Sales. P. C. B., .	83	75		
26	✓	Mdse., ...	" " " . .	58	94		
"	2	J. H. Goldsmith, .	On %, ...			170	
27	✓	Mdse., ...	Petty Sales. P. C. B., .	117	50		
"	2	James Atwater, .	On %, ...			500	
28	✓	Mdse., ...	R. McG. Sales Book, .	156	75		
"	✓	Mdse., ...	Petty Sales. P. C. B., .	87	50		
29	✓	Mdse., ...	" " " . .	112	94		
"	1	Bills Receivable, .	H. Young's note, . . .			750	
	3	Interest, ...	On same, ...			14	50
30	✓	Mdse., ...	Petty Sales. P. C. B., .	175			
	2	*Total to Merchandise,*		2702	27	2702	27
	2	*Total to Cash,*				12397	02

SET IV.

1861 **Cash.** *Cr.*

1861				*Expense.*		*General.*	
Sept.							
1	✓	Expense, ...	Postage Stamps, ...	3			
2	3	Charles Taylor, . .	On %, ...			300	
4	✓	Expense, ...	2 Tons Coal, @ $5, . . .	10			
6	✓	Expense, ...	Bill of Stationery, . . .	15			
"	✓	Expense, ...	Hands, for Shop-work, .	150			
7	2	Mdse., ...	Invoice Cloths. J. B., .			3000	
10	✓	Expense, ...	Gas Bill, ...	15			
13	✓	Expense, ...	Hands, for Shop-work, .	175			
15	3	Bills Payable, . .	Our note, favor H. B., . .			1000	
"	3	Interest, ...	On same, ...			46	75
18	✓	Expense, ...	Clerks' Salaries, ...	112			
20	✓	Expense, ...	Hands, for Shop-work, .	250			
25	✓	Expense, ...	Rent to Sept. 30, ...	100			
26	✓	Expense, ...	Porterage and Drayage, .	35			
28	✓	Expense, ...	Hands, for Shop-work, .	275			
30	✓	Expense, ...	Partners' Salaries to date,	606			
		Total to Expense, ...		1746		1746	
		Total to Cash, ...				6092	75
		BALANCE ON HAND, . . .				6304	27
						12397	02

SALES BOOK,—SET IV.

CHICAGO, SEPTEMBER 1, 1861.

				Cash.		General.	
	THERON W. WOOLSON, *Mt. Pleasant, Ia.*						
	4 Doz. Shirts, 2d quality, 48	@ $1 00	$48 00				
	6 " Union Neckties, 72	" 38¢	27 36				
C.B.	20 " Linen Hdkfs., 240	" 50¢	120 00				
	3 pcs. Cassimere, 150 yds	" 1 25	187 50				
			$382 86				
	Disc. off, 5%		19 14	363	72		
	″						
	IRA PACKARD, *Peru, Ind.,*						
1	50 Boys' overcoats,	@ $5 50	$275 00				
	50 " "	" 7 50	375 00			650	
	B.R. *Note @ 6mo.*						
	3						
	D. V. BELL, *Chicago.*						
	1 Dress suit for self,		$50 00				
C.B.	1 Overcoat for son,		15 00				
	1 Box Hdkfs. 6 doz.	@ $4 00	24 00	89			
	5						
	J. H. GOLDSMITH, *Detroit.*						
2	2 pcs. Eng. B'dc'th, 100 yds	@ $4 00	$400 00				
	50 Military coats, per order,	" 10 00	500 00			900	
	7						
	JAMES ALLEN, *Dubuque.*						
	20 Zouave uniforms,	@ $25 00	$500 00				
C.B.	1 Pce. Stri'd Satin, 50 yds.	" 5 00	250 00				
			$750 00				
	Disc. off Satin, @ 5%		12 50	737	50		
	12						
	JAMES ATWATER, *Madison.*						
	1 Lot ready made clothing viz:						
	10 Coats,	@ $3 00	$30 00				
	20 "	" 3 50	70 00				
2	50 "	" 5 00	250 00				
	8 Pair Pants,	" 3 00	24 00				
	25 " "	" 4 00	100 00				
	50 Vests,	" 1 50	75 00				
	25 "	" 3 00	75 00				
	1 Overcoat,		15 00			639	
				1190	22	2189	00

SALES BOOK,—SET IV.

Chicago, September 15, 1861.

				Cash.		General.	
			Amounts Forward,	1190	22	2189	
	William Baker,		*Springfield.*				
	5 doz. Cravats, 60	@ 75¢	$45 00				
C.B.	3 " " 36	" $1 00	36 00				
	9 " Linen Hdkfs. 108	" 50¢	54 00				
			$135 00				
	Disc. off, 5%		6 75	128	25		
	//						
	J. T. Calkins,		*North Bend, Ind.*				
1	50 Military C'ts, (Privates)	@ $10 00	$500 00				
	5 " " (Officers)	" 15 00	75 00			575	
	18						
	C. D. Bragdon,		*Rock Island.*				
	50 (Ready made) Coats,	@ $5 00	$250 00				
1	100 prs. Pants,	" 3 00	300 00				
	50 doz. Collars,	" 1 50	75 00				
	5 " F. Y. Shirts, 60	" 1 75	105 00			730	
	B.R. *Note @ 6mo.*						
	20						
	George E. Harvey,		*Green Bay.*				
1	100 Zouave Uniforms,	@ $20 00	$2000 00				
	50 Mil. Coats, "Co. H."	" 10 00	500 00			2500	
	B.R. *Note @ 60 ds.*						
	25						
	James W. Lusk,		*Chicago.*				
3	50 Unif'ms ("Linc. Green")	@ $25 00	$1250 00				
	30 " (Zouaves)	" 15 00	450 00			1700	
	28						
	Robert McGrath,		*White Pigeon.*				
	20 (R'dy made) Boy's C'ts,	@ $5 00	$100 00				
C.B.	30 " " Vests,	" 1 50	45 00				
	20 doz. Collars,	" 1 00	20 00				
			$165 00				
	Disc. off 5%		8 25	156	75		
	30						
2	E. R. Felton,		*Peoria.*				
	75 Complete Uniforms,	@ $25 00				1875	
	Sales on time, to credit of Mdse.					9569	
2	Sales for Cash, posted from C.B.			1475	22		
	Petty Sales, entered alone on Cash Book.			1227	05	2702	27
	Total Mdse. sold,					12271	27

LEDGER,—SET IV.

1

Dr. S. S. Packard. *Cr.*

						1861 Sep.	1	By Cash,	CB	5000

Dr. John R. Penn. *Cr.*

1861 Sep.	1	To Bills Payable	J.	1750		1861 Sep.	1	By Mdse.,	J.	6750

Dr. J. C. Bryant. *Cr.*

1861 Sep.	1	To Sundries,	J.	900		1861 Sep.	1	By Sundries,	J.	5900

Dr. Bills Receivable. *Cr.*

1861 Sep.	1	To J. C. Bryant,	J.	1500		1861 Sep.	17	By Cash,	CB	750
"	20	" P.C.Schuyler	J.	1104		"	29	" "	CB	750
"	1	" Mdse.,	SB	650						
"	18	" "	SB	730						
"	20	" "	SB	2500						

Dr. J. T. Calkins. *Cr.*

1861 Sep.	1	To J. C. Bryant,	J.	500		1861 Sep.	2	By Cash,	CB	200
"	15	" Mdse.,	SB	575		"	16	" "	CB	150

Dr. Cash. *Cr.*

1861						1861					
Sep.	30	To Sundries,	CB	12397	02	Sep.	30	By Sundries,	CB	6092	75

Dr. Merchandise. *Cr.*

1861						1861					
Sep.	1	To J. R. Penn,	J.	6750		Sep.	30	By Cash,	CB	2702	27
"	7	" Cash,	CB	3000		"	"	" Sundries,	SB	9560	

Dr. E. R. Felton. *Cr.*

1861						1861					
Sep.	1	To J. C. Bryant,	J.	376		Sep.	25	By Cash,	CB	376	
"	30	" Mdse.,	SB	1875							

Dr. J. H. Goldsmith. *Cr.*

1861						1861					
Sep.	1	To J. C. Bryant,	J.	1170		Sep.	22	By Cash,	CB	1000	
"	5	" Mdse.,	SB	900		"	26	" "	CB	170	

Dr. James Atwater. *Cr.*

1861						1861					
Sep.	1	To J. C. Bryant,	J.	1250		Sep.	10	By Cash,	CB	750	
"	12	" Mdse.,	SB	639		"	27	" "	CB	500	

Dr. P. C. Schuyler. *Cr.*

Date				Amount		Date				Amount	
1861 Sep.	1	To J. C. Bryant,	J.	1104		1861 Sep.	20	By Bills Rec'ble	J.	1104	

Dr. Charles Taylor. *Cr.*

Date				Amount		Date				Amount	
1861 Sep.	2	To Cash,	CB	300		1861 Sep.	1	By J. C. Bryant,	J.	500	

Dr. James W. Lusk. *Cr.*

Date				Amount		Date				Amount	
1861 Sep.	15	To Bills Payable	J.	400		1861 Sep.	1	By J. C. Bryant,	J.	400	
"	25	" Mdse.,	SB	1700							

Dr. Bills Payable. *Cr.*

Date				Amount		Date				Amount	
1861 Sep.	15	To Cash,	CB	1000		1861 Sep.	1	By J. R. Penn,	J.	1750	
						"	15	" J. W. Lusk,	J.	400	

Dr. Interest. *Cr.*

Date				Amount		Date				Amount	
1861 Sep.	15	To Cash,	CB	46	75	1861 Sep.	17	By Cash,	CB	34	25
						"	29	" "	CB	14	50

LEDGER,—SET IV.

4

Dr. Expense. *Cr.*

1861. Sep.	30	To Cash,	CB	1746						

EXERCISES FOR THE LEARNER.

FOURTH SERIES.

THE following routine is a continuation of the business of Set IV, and the transactions should be entered in the proper books and posted in accordance with the plan and instructions of the Set, using the same books, and producing at the close, a general result of the whole business. As this set is by far the most practical in the treatise, its peculiar points should be thoroughly impressed upon the mind. The student should exercise much care in the symmetrical arrangement of the original Books of Entry. The accompanying initials will indicate the books to be written up, and their order.

Memoranda.

October 1. Bo't of Dunham & Brokaw on %, Invoice of Mdse. amounting to $6000, (J.)—Sold James Johnson, Freeport, for Cash, 1 doz. Fancy Neckties, @ $1 each; 12 doz. prs. Lisle Thread Stockings, @ $3 per doz., (S.B., C.B.)—**2.** Paid Shop-hands, Cash, $300, (C.B.)—Received Cash for Petty Sales, $119, (C.B.)—**3.** Received Cash of J. H. Goldsmith, in full of %, $900, (C.B.)—Sold E. R. Felton, on %, 6 doz. French Yoke Shirts, @ $18 per doz.; 10 doz. Knit Undershirts, @ $7 per doz.; 8 doz. pr. Knit Drawers, @ $8 per doz., (S.B.)—**5.** Received Cash for Petty Sales, $120, (C.B.)—Sold Robert Harmer, Vandalia, for Cash, 15 Summer Coats, @ $2; 20 do. Vests, @ $1 50; 6 doz. Cut-throat Collars, @ $2 per doz., (C.B.)—**7.** Paid Cash for repairing store, $150, (C.B.)—Received Cash for Petty Sales, $94 83, (C.B.)—**8.** Received Cash of J. T. Calkins, in full of %, $725, (C.B.)—Sold Jacob Horn, Milwaukee, on his note @ 60 ds., 50 Complete Uniforms, @ $20, (S.B.)—Received Cash for Petty Sales, $110, (C.B.)—**9.** Paid Shop-hands, Cash, $297, (C.B.)—Sold J. W. Lusk, on %, 2 doz. Ready made Coats, 24 @ $5; 15 prs. Pants, @ $3 75; 30 Vests, @ $2; 1 Fine Overcoat, $25, (S.B.)—**10.** Received Cash for Petty Sales, $119 50, (C.B.)—**12.** Received Cash in full for P. C. Schuyler's note, $1104, (C.B.)—**15.** Sold Abraham Jackson for Cash, 5 doz. Byron Collars, @ $2 per doz.; 4 doz. D'Orsay Cravats, @ $12 per doz., (S.B.,C.B.)—Received Cash for Petty Sales, $157 30, (C.B.) —**16.** Paid Dunham & Brokaw, Cash on %, $3000, (C.B.)—Paid Shop-hands, Cash, $263, (C.B.)—Received Cash for Petty Sales, $85 90, (C.B.)—**18.** Sold E. R. Felton, on %, 1 Case Overalls, 6 doz. prs. @ $6 per doz.; 2 Cases Summer Frocks, 12 doz. @ $18 per doz., (S.B.)—Received Cash for Petty Sales, $115, (C.B.)—**20.** Received Cash of E. R. Felton on %, $1500, (C.B.)—Sold Robert C. Spencer, St. Louis, for Cash, 10 Military Coats, @ $15; 5 do. (officers,) @ $25, (S.B., C.B.)—Received Cash for Petty Sales, $143, (C.B.)—**21.** Paid Cash for salaries, $117, (C.B.)—Sold Chas. Taylor, on %, 1 Piece French Cassimere, 50 yds. @ $3, (S.B.) Received Cash for Petty Sales, $125, (C.B.)—Paid Dunham & Brokaw, Cash in full of %, $3000, (C.B.)—**23.** Paid Shop-hands, Cash, $375, (C.B.)—Received Cash for Petty Sales, $75, (C.B.)—**25.** Sold James Atwater, on %, 1 doz. Boy's Frocks, 12, @ $2; 3 doz. do., 36, @ $5, (S.B.)—Received Cash for Petty Sales, $85 90, (C.B.)—**27.** Received Cash of James Atwater, in full of %, $843, (C.B.)—**28.** Paid Cash for Gas Bill, $15; Rent, $100, (C.B.)—**30.** Paid Shop-hands, Cash $400, (C.B.)

STATEMENT.

The above transactions properly entered will produce the following result.

	Face of Ledger.				Balances.			
	Dr.		*Cr.*		*Dr.*		*Cr.*	
S. S. Packard, ...			5000				5000	
J. R. Penn, ...	1750		6750				5000	
J. C. Bryant, ...	900		5900				5000	
Bills Receivable, ...	7484		2604		4880			
Cash, ...	19272	45	14109	75	5162	70		
Merchandise, ...	15750		16183	95			433	95
E. R. Felton, ...	2745		1876		869			
Charles Taylor, ...	450		500				50	
J. W. Lusk, ...	2361	25	400		1961	25		
Bills Payable, ...	1000		2150				1150	
Interest, ...	46	75	48	75			2	
Expense, ...	3763				3763			
	55522	45	55522	45	16635	95	16635	95

PRACTICAL HINTS

FOR TEACHER AND PUPIL.

In the preparation of this book the authors have kept in view one important fact, viz: that in order to become a practical accountant, the student should learn not only to *think for himself*, but to give his thoughts appropriate form and expression; hence the introduction of intermediate "Exercises for the Learner," and "Examples for Practice," intended to throw him upon his own resources, and rescue him from the too common error of copying. We feel sure that this feature will commend itself to all who use the book, and especially to the faithful teacher who is satisfied with no progress which is not real. The three qualities essential to success in Accountantship are, 1. Accuracy; 2. Neatness; 3. Dispatch; and these are to be acquired only through *practice.* Instead therefore, of omitting any of the practical Exercises, or passing lightly over them, they should be regarded as vital and indispensable, and should they not afford sufficient practice, additional exercises should be given by the teacher or self-imposed by the student. The limited space afforded' renders it impossible to carry out in detail, all the labor which actual business would require in the way of filling out notes, drafts, checks, etc., or to suggest appropriate forms for such letters and documents as would be necessary in conducting the business represented; but the student should be required to supply this deficiency, with such aid as the teacher may think prudent to offer.

The following brief hints may afford some assistance in carrying out the intention of the work.

ORDER AND NEATNESS.

There is no error more fatal to the student in Accounts than the impression which so generally prevails, that a theoretical knowledge of general principles will prepare him for the duties of the Counting Room. It is true that *without* this knowledge, he need never hope to succeed; and equally true that with it, *alone*, he will be quite as unfortunate. Although in enumerating the neccessary qualifications of an Accountant we have placed neatness, *second* in the list, it is the *first* which attracts attention, and is of the utmost importance in establishing a reputation for practical accountantship. Neatness, in Book-keeping is the result of *good writing* and *tasteful arrangement.* It is a mistaken idea conceived by ambitious youth and fostered by peripatetic writing masters, that the ability to form a few wondrous curves in the execution of capital letters, or the adornment of a fancy title constitutes the chief qualification of a business writer. Practical men are not apt to appreciate qualifications of this kind, but insist, rather, on the utmost modesty of display and simplicity of arrangement. A professional *flourish* is as much out of place on a page of business record, as a daub of oil color on a marble statue. Uniformity, legibility, and adaptation to space and purpose should be the characteristics of business writing; and he who fails in these essentials will need something more than a certificate from some professor of the art to save him from just condemnation. These strictures are not in disparagement to any style or system of penmanship, nor designed to underrate the profession which lends such a charm to our thoughts by setting them in graceful symbols; but to exalt the *practical* above the *fanciful;* and to insist upon a proper recognition of the standard of taste which the experience and observation of business men have adopted. Rapidity of execution is an essential element in business writing, but even this should be subordinated to neatness. In the selection of script for the principal forms in Part I. reference has been had to the standard of neatness above indicated. It is not expected that the student will attempt to copy the *style* of the writing, but it is hoped that he may seek to emulate its legibility and taste in arrangement. Particularly should he exercise great care in avoiding errors which will necessitate erasures. Nothing so destroys the beauty of a page as erasures and interlineations. Even occasional *blotting* is preferable to occasional *scratching.* Where it is possible, errors should be corrected by counter entries, thus affording an explanation, without destroying the harmony of the page. Finally let the student practice until he becomes proficient in *ruling.* In using red ink great care should be had to keep it pure; and to that end, it is never allowable to use a pen that has been dipped in black. Even steel pens are thought to destroy the brilliancy of red ink, and quills are preferred on that account. A steel pen, however, is the best for ruling, and needs only to be kept perfectly clean. For ruling with a common steel pen, no rule is so convenient as the *round,* but to use it skilfully requires much practice, and a steady hand.

PROFICIENCY IN MATHEMATICS.

The processes of Book-keeping seldom call into practice the higher departments of mathematics; albeit a thorough mathematician—other things being equal—will make the best accountant. The kind of proficiency most available to a Book-keeper is facility and accuracy in addition. The ability to add long columns of figures with speed and certainty is one of the very best claims a young man can present for a position of trust. So highly is this accomplishment esteemed by business men, that where it is wanting other qualifications sink into comparative insignificance. A clerk who "*never makes a mistake*" is sure of promotion and remuneration. There are many theories as to the surest and most rapid method of adding, and occasionally some eccentric genius electrifies the world with an exhibition of almost magical power in this direction; but the only thing that can with safety be relied upon is *practice*—faithful and continued *practice.* The student should be required to write down long columns of figures of various numerical values, and test his powers by adding, first in one direction and then in the other; occasionally trying two and three columns at a time. We give below three simple processes of retaining the figure to be *carried*—a very important matter with beginners. The first is the usual method of writing the carrying figure *small* under the unit amount of the column which produced it. The second requires the addition of each separate column to be written down on a waste space commencing with the right hand column and carrying to the next as in the usual method; these separate amounts placed in their order one under the other will present in their unit figures, counting upward, the general result. The third method consists of the proper arrangement of the independent sum of each column, so that, being added, the proper result is secured.

EXAMPLES.

First Process.

1829	25
743	18
2562	28
145	19
2823	25
7574	28
4291	83
25	64
19994	90
333	25

Second Process.

1st column,		50
2d	"	29
3d	"	34
4th	"	39
5th	"	39
6th	"	19 994 90

Third Process.

					5	0
				2	4	:
			3	2	:	:
		3	6	:	:	:
	3	6	:	:	:	:
1	6	:	:	:	:	:
1	9	9	9	4	9	0

The process of adding two or more columns at once is much more simple than is generally supposed; requiring little, if any, more skill than the common method The only point of difficulty is the necessity of adding units to units, tens to tens, etc. To give the student an idea of the process, we will take the two cent-columns in the above example, and add them together. Commencing with the lower amount, we proceed: 64 and 3 are 67, and 80 are 147, and 8 are 155, and 20 are 175, and 5 are 180, and 20 are 200, and 9 are 209, and 10 are 219, and 8 are 227, and 20 are 247, and 8 are 255, and 10 are 265, and 5 are 270, and 20 are 290; which is the sum of the two columns. It will be seen that we separate each amount into units and tens, adding the units to the units and the tens to the tens of the accumulating result. We will now vary the process by commencing at the top and adding downward; and also by adding the tens first: 25 and 10 are 35, and 8 are 43, and 20 are 63, and 8 are 71, and 10 are 81, and 9 are 90, and 20 are 110, and 5 are 115, and 20 are 135, and 8 are 143, and 80 are 223, and 3 are 226, and 60 are 286, and 4 are 290; the same result as before. By continued practice of this kind the student will soon be able to astonish himself with his own proficiency. Let him practice on *two* columns, until he becomes thoroughly familiar with the process, and then take three, and four. The necessity of keeping his mind constantly on the alert for fear of adding tens to units, and units to hundreds, will serve to quicken his powers of concentration, and develop the practical resources of his mind.

TO DETECT ERRORS IN THE TRIAL BALANCE.

Undoubtedly the best method for guarding against the trouble of finding errors in the Trial Balance is *not to make* them; but as this advice is much more easily given than followed, and as, in despite of the best efforts, Trial Balances do frequently fail to equilibrate, a few hints as to the most approved methods of discovering the errors may be kindly received. In the first place let it be remembered that while the Trial Balance is not a *sure test* of the correctness of the Ledger, no Double Entry Ledger *can be* correct that does not balance; hence, the necessity of knowing that the sides are equal. The Trial Balance is simply the summing up of the debit and credit sides of the Ledger to ascertain if they are equal. If the trial should prove that they are *not* equal, the cause must exist either in entries being omitted, posted to the wrong side, or in wrong amounts. A little observation will enable the accountant to classify the error under one of the above heads. If the precaution indicated in our first Double Entry sets be taken, viz: to carry the total amounts posted into the Trial Balance—and either side agrees with the footing of the Journal columns, the difficulty is easily overcome, as the difference between the sides will show not only the error or combination of errors, but the *side* of the Ledger upon which they occur. For various reasons, however, it is not always convenient to embrace the total Ledger entries in the Trial Balance:—therefore for general purposes, we would suggest the following process for detecting errors: *First*, make sure that an error exists. It is often the case that an overweening anxiety to have the sides of the Trial Balance equal actually produces a *supposititious* error, by dissipating the mind while engaged in ascertaining the result, and thus persistently, though erroneously realizing its own fears, by errors in addition. If an error *seems* to exist, before attempting to find it, go carefully over the work of addition, proving it in every way. If the test should prove that the sides do not equal, refer to the Ledger accounts, and ascertain that the proper amounts have been transferred to the Trial Balance. Foot up the accounts very carefully, and permit no doubt to exist that the exact *condition* of the Ledger is shown in the Trial Balance.—*Second*, If the error still exists, ascertain its *exact amount*, and then look carefully for the same amount in the Journal, which may have been omitted in posting. If no such an amount should appear, or should not prove to have been omitted, next ascertain if any Journal Entry exists of *half* the amount, which being posted to the *wrong side* would produce the difference. Should this test prove unsuccessful, ascertain if the difference be divisible by 9, and if so, look carefully for a transposition of some amount posted.*—*Third*, Should this process fail the last resort is to *check* the postings. First ascertain that the Journal entries balance and then go carefully over the work, checking in pencil mark, all entries that have been properly posted both on the Journal and the Ledger. The most reliable process of checking is to have one person take the Journal and call off the Ledger titles and amounts, slowly and distinctly—the debits first, and credits next—while another examines the Ledger entries to see if they correspond. Many practical accountants adopt the plan of thus checking before attempting to take a Trial Balance, for the purpose, not only of facilitating the labor but of being assured that the Ledger is absolutely correct. *We cordially commend the practice*, believing that if it is adopted, and faithfully carried out there will be little need of resorting to any other method to ensure a balance. Above all, *let the student hunt up his own errors* of balance; for while it is true that all such errors are the result of careless-

* It is a curious fact that the difference between any given amount composed of two or more figures, and the same figures transposed, is divisible by 9. For example, the difference between 75 and 57 is 18; between 120 and 210, 90; between 195 and 159, 36; etc., all of which differences 18, 90, and 36, are divisible by nine, without a remainder. The illustration may be carried to any extent, with the same results.

ness, the adoption of means to detect them, will tend, in the greatest degree to perfect his mind in those practical questions and labor, necessary to the full development of his powers. It is the duty of the teacher to open up to the pupil's mind the bearings of the various principles of the science he would inculcate, as well as to aid him in the application of those principles; but *practical results* should be the student's own work. For these he should be held responsible; and should never be allowed to fall into the loose habit of making errors that his teacher may find them.

RESOURCES AND LIABILITIES.

These terms are used extensively in this work, and their importance in properly defining the condition of the business has been forcibly set before the student. He has been taught that certain Ledger accounts are used to show resources, and certain others to show liabilities, and that the correspondence between the resources and liabilities thus shown must agree in a certain sense, with the accounts showing gains and losses. Any careful observer, however, must be aware that all classes of resources are not equally valuable; and that, in the course of trade, persons may become indebted to us both on note and account who will *never* pay; the resource thus represented being absolutely valueless. In estimating the condition of a concern, therefore, it is well to know whether the books are *truthful*; that is whether the *resources* exhibited on their pages are absolute or fictitious. (The *liabilities* are always presumed to be genuine.) The importance of this precaution will be apparent when we consider that all gains in business, as shown by *representative* accounts, are predicated upon the integrity of the resources. For instance, suppose we sell A, $500 worth of Merchandise, and take his note for it. In recording the transaction, we credit Merchandise, and debit Bills Receivable. In estimating our gains and losses, we, of course include among the proceeds of Merchandise this amount, which adds $500 to our gains. Our Merchandise account is closed, and the result finds its way into the Loss and Gain account, thus having an important bearing upon the apparent prosperity of the business. But suppose this note should prove *worthless*. It is now evident that the $500 credited to Merchandise account was not a legitimate product, and that all gains predicated upon it are necessarily fictitious. But there are other resources represented in the Ledger, the exact value of which is *uncertain*,—they may be worth their face, or half of it, or *nothing*. How shall they be treated in a general exposition of affairs? Should we consider them all valueless, and close them into Loss and Gain, the error may be as great as to permit them to remain and represent actual worth. The most approved method of disposing of this class of accounts, is to permit them to remain upon the Ledger, but to neutralize their effect by opening an account showing fictitious liabilities of the same amount. An appropriate title for this account is "Suspense." When therefore doubtful resources exist on our Ledger, and we do not wish to represent anything more than *actual* gains, the process should be to debit Loss and Gain, and credit "Suspense" with the amount of the doubtful resources. If any of these are afterwards paid, or their value becomes tangible, it is very easy to restore them by debiting Suspense and crediting Loss and Gain. This method is far preferable to the more usual one of *closing* up all doubtful accounts into Suspense. The Suspense account in the latter case would represent either a loss or a resource. If a loss the amount may as well go at once to the Loss and Gain account; and if a resource, it had much better remain under its own more appropriate title. But the chief objection to this course would be the exhibiting of accounts as closed, which are yet owing and may be paid. If Mr. A, for instance, whom we thus consider doubtful, should desire to see his account in our Ledger, that he may pay it, it might be awkward to inform him that, having considered his account worthless we had carried it to Loss and Gain. He might not desire to change our estimate of the value of his indebtedness.

EXCHANGE.

Exchange is a term used to denote that commercial usage by which individuals are enabled to cancel debts at a distance without the transmission of money. This is effected through a species of commercial paper known as "Bills of Exchange."

A Bill of Exchange is a written order addressed to a person directing the payment of a certain sum of money, either upon its presentation, or at a specified time thereafter. There are two classes of Exchange, *domestic* and *foreign*.

DOMESTIC EXCHANGE consists of drafts, notes, checks, certificates of deposits, etc., the parties to which reside in the same country.

FOREIGN EXCHANGE is usually represented by drafts, the parties to which reside in different countries. They are usually drawn in *sets* of three or more, one of which being honored, the others become void. The separate bills are sent by different routes, or at different times, and the first that comes to hand, if either, is honored. Foreign Bills of Exchange are made payable in the currency of the country upon which they are drawn, instead of that where they originate.

FORM OF A SET OF EXCHANGE.

—1.—

EXCHANGE FOR £1000. *New York, July* 1, 1861.

Ten days after sight of this my *first* Bill of Exchange, (second and third of same date and tenor unpaid) pay to S. S. Packard or order, One Thousand Pounds Sterling, value received, with or without further advice.

H. D. STRATTON.

To GEORGE PEABODY & Co.
Bankers, London.

—2.—

EXCHANGE FOR £1000. *New-York, July* 1, 1861.

Ten days after sight of this my *second* Bill of Exchange, (first and third of same date and tenor unpaid) pay to S. S. Packard or order, One Thousand Pounds Sterling, value received, with or without further advice.

H. D. STRATTON.

To GEORGE PEABODY & Co.
Bankers, London.

—3.—

EXCHANGE FOR £1000. *New-York, July* 1, 1861.

Ten days after sight of this my *third* Bill of Exchange, (first and second of same date and tenor unpaid) pay to S. S. Packard or order, One Thousand Pounds Sterling, value received, with or without further advice.

H. D. STRATTON.

To GEORGE PEABODY & Co.
Bankers, London.

FORMS OF NOTES, DRAFTS, CHECKS, ETC.

The following forms of notes, drafts, checks, receipts, etc., comprise the great bulk of business paper entering into the various departments of domestic trade.

Notes.

1. *Individual Note.*

NEW-YORK, *July* 1, 1861.

$500.

One day after date, I promise to pay M. B. Scott or order, Five Hundred Dollars, value received.

JACOB HINDS.

2. *Joint Note.*

BUFFALO, *May* 1, 1861.

$1000.

Sixty days after date, we promise to pay N. C. Winslow, or order, at New-York and Erie Bank, One Thousand Dollars, value received.

J. C. BRYANT,
W. P. SPENCER.

3. *Joint and Several Note, (with interest.)*

CLEVELAND, *January* 10, 1861.

$1500.

One month after date, we or either of us promise to pay John R. Penn or order, Fifteen Hundred Dollars, value received with interest from date.

E. G. FOLSOM,
E. R. FELTON,

4. *Principal and Surety Note.*

CHICAGO, *July* 10, 1861.

$600.

Thirty days after date, I promise to pay James Richards or order, Six Hundred Dollars, value received.

H. B. BRYANT, *Principal.*
E. B. ROCKWELL, *Surety.*

5. *Chattel Note.*

DETROIT, *April* 12, 1861.

$400.

Three months from date, for value received, I promise to pay to John Jones or order, Four Hundred Dollars, in Pine Lumber, at the then market rate, the same to be delivered as per his order, within the limits of the city of Detroit.

HENRY P. SMITH.

6. *Non-negotiable Note.*

$375. ALBANY, *June* 10, 1861.

One month from date, I promise to pay James Cruikshank, Three Hundred and Seventy Five Dollars at his office.

W. H. CLARK.

Drafts.

1. *Time reckoned from sight.*

$500. PHILADELPHIA, *June* 12, 1861.

At ten days' sight, pay to the order of Daniel Slote, Five Hundred Dollars, value received, and charge to account of

L. FAIRBANKS.

To PACKARD & PENN,
18 Cooper Inst. N.Y.

2. *Reckoned from Date.*

$750. WASHINGTON, D.C. *April* 28, 1861.

Ten days after date, pay to Austin Packard or order, Seven Hundred and Fifty Dollars, value received, and charge to my account.

ZALMON RICHARDS.

To IVISON, PHINNEY & Co.
48 Walker St., N.Y.

Due Bills.

1. *For Cash, Drawing Interest.*

$175 $\frac{33}{100}$. ST. LOUIS, *July* 1, 1861.

Due Henry C. Spencer, on demand, One Hundred and Seventy Five $\frac{33}{100}$ Dollars, with interest from date.

WM. H. BEEBE,

2. *For Merchandise, without Interest.*

$100. CINCINNATI, *June* 12, 1861.

Due R. M. Bartlett, One Hundred Dollars, payable in Wheat, at market price, on the first day of September next.

WILLIAM MOORE.

Orders.

1. *To apply on Account.*

BALTIMORE, *April* 12, 1861.

Mr. J. Austin Sperry will please pay to the bearer, Fifty Dollars, in Merchandise, on my account.

J. D. HINDE.

2. *In full of Account.*

GRANVILLE, O., *Sept.* 10, 1861.

THOMAS PEASE, ESQ.

Please pay to John McDonald or bearer, One Hundred Dollars, from your store, and this shall be your receipt in full of my account.

JAMES G. IRWIN.

Receipts.

1. *On Account.*

$400.—Received, January 1, 1861, Four Hundred Dollars, on account of James W. Lusk.

S. C. GRIGGS & Co.

2. *In full of all demands.*

$575. ROCHESTER, *June* 19, 1861.

Received of Geo. W. Eastman, Five Hundred and Seventy-five Dollars, in full of all demands.

D. W. FISH.

3. *To apply on Contract.*

$1000. SYRACUSE, *Jan.* 12, 1861.

Received of S. M. Bassett, One Thousand Dollars, the same to apply on contract for building house, dated Jan. 1, 1861.

ROBERT WALLACE.

4. *To apply as an Endorsement.*

$75. *July* 10, 1861.

Received on the within note, Seventy-five Dollars.

JAMES SMITH.

5. *Receipt for Property.*

NEW-YORK, *Jan.* 15, 1861.

Received of Duncan Phyfe, the following enumerated articles to be held in trust for him, and returned on his demand: one Gold Watch (Hunting case), two Promissory notes, each dated Jan. 1, 1861, and signed by William Prentiss—one for Three Hundred Dollars, due in six months from date, and one for Five Hundred Dollars, due in eight months from date.

S. S. PACKARD.

Checks.

1. *Payable to Bearer.*

$100. MERCANTILE BANK, NEW-YORK, *May* 10, 1861.

Pay to John Doe or Bearer, One Hundred Dollars.

(No. 1963.) PETER COOPER.

2. *Payable to Order.*

$300. MERCANTILE BANK, NEW-YORK, *April* 10, 1861.

Pay to Charles Strong or Order, Three Hundred Dollars.

PETER COOPER.

Certificate of Deposit.

$500. EXCHANGE BANK, ALBANY, MARCH 1, 1861.

J. T. Calkins has deposited in this Bank, Five Hundred Dollars, payable to C. C. Conant or Order, on return of this certificate.

(No. 1900.) CHAS. EDDY, *Teller.*

QUESTIONS FOR REVIEW.

REMARKS, PAGE 172.

1. In what consists the peculiarity of Set IV? 2. How have the transactions been entered heretofore? 3. What objection to entering all the transactions in the Journal? 4. What advantage in posting from the original books of entry? 5. What difficulty in the way? 6. How do you avoid posting certain entries *twice?* 7. When are the amounts in the "General" column to be posted? 8. When the special columns? 9. What reference is made in the Ledger to the book from which the several amounts are posted?

PRACTICAL HINTS, PAGE 183.

10. What *three* qualifications are necessary to good accountantship? 11. How are these to be acquired? 12. In what does *neatness* in Bookkeeping consist? 13. What are the characteristics of good business writing? 14. What is said of *rapidity?* 15. What of errors and omissions? 16. Interlineations and Erasures? 17. What precautions should be observed in the use of red ink? 18. What kind of mathematical proficiency is most available to the Bookkeeper? 19. How is facility in addition to be acquired? 20. What is the process of adding two or three columns at once? 21. What is the *best* method of avoiding the difficulties in getting a Trial Balance? 22. Is the Trial Balance a *sure test* of the correctness of the Ledger? 23. What is a Trial Balance? 24. Will you give the processes for discovering an error in the Trial Balance? 25. What curious fact connected with the transposition of figures? 26. What plan is recommended to guard against *fictitious* gains? 27. What does the "Suspense" account show? 28. What is meant by Exchange? 29. What is a Bill of Exchange? 30. Of what does Domestic Exchange consist? 31. Foreign Exchange? 32. How are Foreign bills drawn? 33. Why in Sets? 34. In what currency are they payable?

Henry C Ripley
Saginaw City
Oct 16th 1865